Presented To:

_____

From:

_____

Date:

_____

PATHWAYS TO HEALING:
Overcoming Childhood Trauma and Adult Pain of Sibling Estrangement

Copyright © 2021 by Carmen Carrol Enterprise

Published by Carmen Carrol Enterprise

ISBN 978-1-7398859-0-8

All rights reserved. This book or any portion thereof may not be reproduced or used in any manner whatsoever, without the express written permission of the publisher.

Printed in the United Kingdom

Scripture quotations are from Bible Hub (biblehub.com), using the following versions:

New International Version (NIV)

English Standard Version (ESV)

New King James Version (NKJV)

New Living Translation (NLT)

Cover design and layout by miadesign.com

Disclaimer:
This is my story, and I am sharing it to the best of my knowledge and ability. I don't claim to be a Doctor or a Psychologist. I do claim to be a survivor of Childhood Trauma and Adult Pain. The experience that I have gone through has impacted my life, so I want to encourage and help others who may have gone through a similar thing.

PATHWAYS TO HEALING

Overcoming Childhood Trauma and
Adult Pain of Sibling Estrangement

CARMEN CARROL

LIFE AND SUCCESS PUBLISHING
www.abookinsideyou.com

PATHWAYS TO HEALING:
Overcoming Childhood Trauma and Adult Pain of Sibling Estrangement

*"Then you will know the truth,
and the truth will set you free."*
John 8:32^(NIV)

Maze: 'a network of paths and hedges designed
as a puzzle, through which one has to find a way.'
(dictionary.cambridge.org)

PATHWAYS TO HEALING:
Overcoming Childhood Trauma and Adult Pain of Sibling Estrangement

CONTENTS

Introduction 13
Preface 19
Chapter One: When You Think About It 23
Chapter Two: Family Feuds Has Roots 41
Chapter Three: Childhood Trauma and Adult Pain 55
Chapter Four: The R-Word - Rejection 63
Chapter Five: Honour 71
Chapter Six: Tag, You Are Next 75
Chapter Seven: Blame & Shame 81
Chapter Eight: Casting Aside Imaginations 87
Chapter Nine: Whole in Every Part 93
Chapter Ten: Power in a Name 101
Chapter Eleven: I Am 107
Chapter Twelve: Character Building Equals Pain 113
Chapter Thirteen: Joseph & Jesus Comparisons 119
Chapter Fourteen: Joseph Sold by his Brothers 125
Chapter Fifteen: Seeing Through the Eyes of Purpose 133
Chapter Sixteen: Sum of Three Parts 141
Chapter Seventeen: Depression 147
Chapter Eighteen: Plan of Action 153
Chapter Nineteen: Weights & Baggage 159

PATHWAYS TO HEALING:
Overcoming Childhood Trauma and Adult Pain of Sibling Estrangement

Chapter Twenty: You are Unique... 167

Chapter Twenty-One: It's working for Your Good 173

Chapter Twenty-Two: Dealing with Rejection 179

Chapter Twenty-Three: This Square Peg Does Not Fit 189

Chapter Twenty-Four: Relationship Challenges 195

Chapter Twenty-Five: Silent Voices, Hear Me Roar 201

Chapter Twenty-Six: Truth Be Told 209

Chapter Twenty-Seven: Pathways to Healing 215

About the Author 229

Index 231

DEDICATION

First, I want to give thanks to God for giving me the strength to go through a very difficult time in my life. For walking with me through the pain, even when I could not feel Him close by. For reminding me that He knew the end from the beginning through the assurance of Scripture.

"...For I know the plans I have for you," declares the LORD, "plans to prosper you and not to harm you, plans to give you hope and a future..." – Jeremiah 29:11(NIV)

To my husband, Mel, for your unconditional love, and for supporting me as I walked on my journey towards healing. You relentlessly believed in me and always gave me the encouragement to fulfil my dreams.

To those of you who have experienced the pain of sibling rejection and estrangement, I want you to know I see you, I hear you, and I know you will make it because there is an appointed time for your healing!

PATHWAYS TO HEALING:
Overcoming Childhood Trauma and Adult Pain of Sibling Estrangement

BOOK REVIEWS

Here is what people are saying about Pathways to Healing.

*"It is impossible for someone to read this book and not be **encouraged**, delivered and transformed. I highly recommend Pathways to Healing; you will be blessed."* **R.Daley – Daley Bread Productions, Birmingham, UK**

*"I found this to be a **very frank** and moving story of the life of a woman who deeply cares about the well-being and development of others. Through her own experience of hurt and feelings of rejection, growing up in her own family led to her feeling unworthy of love and also impacted her ability to trust others, especially men. Having found her own pathways to healing through her relationship with God, she shares this with others.*

Her story is one that many will be able to relate to. Throughout the book, she uses stories and readings from the Bible to give hope and encouragement. She warns about the danger of holding on to hurt and anger, as this itself can develop into emotional problems with possible physical health consequences. Her use of exercises to help the readers reflect on their personal experiences and, in so doing, identify a way towards healing that is poignant and helpful. The use of the story of Joseph and his treatment by his brothers and also his later life experiences

PATHWAYS TO HEALING:
Overcoming Childhood Trauma and Adult Pain of Sibling Estrangement

give further hope that God uses all our experiences for his ***greater purpose****. Carmen's illustrations of her poetry and the encouragement from her to find someone we can trust to talk to serves to highlight a pathway to self-healing for those who are struggling with that too common human condition. Finally, she reminds us all that we are made for* **LOVE***.*" **Catherine Lecointe - Therapist & Counsellor, Bristol, UK**

"*On a personal note, I've learned a lot about myself and* ***you've inspired*** *me to look into some things, so thank you!*" **Esther. W Kiburi, - Editor, Gillingham, UK**

INTRODUCTION

Are you a dreamer, just like Joseph in the Bible? Are you carefree and enjoying your life? The story of Joseph is full of all the components for a heartfelt story; you have the loveable character, the villain, the conflict, the emotional rollercoaster of betrayal, rejection, forgiveness and reconciliation... His story is also a well-known musical, *Joseph and the Amazing Technicolour Dreamcoat*, which has been showcased in theatres around the world.

This journey took seventeen years to unfold. I love the story of Joseph. I can understand to some extent what he must have gone through and felt, whilst going through so much pain inflicted by the actions of some of his siblings.

I also go into more details about my story, and I will share with you what I learned along the way when dealing with sibling rejection from a young age. My story would be incomplete if I did not mention Joseph. The impact of his story - of overcoming the difficulties he had with his family - continues to influence me to this day, and I'm so grateful for it! I go into more details about his story throughout the book, and share some of the principles that I've learnt along the way, that I think you will benefit from. Joseph's story is the backdrop I wanted to create, so that I could share my own story of sibling estrangement. So, where did it start?

PATHWAYS TO HEALING:
Overcoming Childhood Trauma and Adult Pain of Sibling Estrangement

Here I was, a shy, creative and sensitive child, who went through a kind of pain - one that is hard to explain - when I was growing up. To become a survivor of childhood trauma and now an author is still amazing to me.

Throughout these pages, I will share and be vulnerable about the relationship challenges I've faced in my life. So, let me start by saying that when we think about sibling rivalry, what normally comes to mind are the everyday growing pains we all go through as children. There is the regular banter that goes on, the constant competing with one another and, of course, the fights, the bullying, and wanting to be the first and the best. But my story is different. Of course, I experienced all the above, but there were extra loads and challenges I did not know I had to face and overcome. Unfortunately, my story has resulted in me being estranged from some of my siblings, which makes me so sad and disappointed that I can't even put it into words. My life started to change between the tender ages of five and six, which, according to raisingchildren.net.au, are our formative years, when our identity and character are established. During that time, life decided to take me on the rollercoaster ride of survival, self-discovery, pain, rejection, abandonment and uncertainties about my identity. This journey was full of highs and lots of lows; the ride was hard and has not stopped. Now that I'm an adult, I had to decide to change whilst still in the midst of the storm swirling around me.

INTRODUCTION

What a long time! I hear you say, and I agree with you. You can understand, then, that I've felt very reluctant to share my story (if I'm honest), because it was an experience I had walked through mostly alone, and it has cost me greatly! In saying that, it has contributed to my growth and character; negatively and positively. Once as a friendly, happy person, I was becoming a person who was angry, resentful and disappointed with life for such a long time. This was not the real me, though. The pain I went through had hidden the real me! There, I've said it. I was being hidden by my pain for so long I did not know what living a full life looked like anymore, so why on earth would I want others to know about it, right? But I thought about it, and I sensed that living a full life was for others. So my reaction to that was, "Oh, it was for others, but what about *me*?"

When looking at our past experiences - if they have been filled with trauma or any form of abuse - be it physical, emotional, sexual or spiritual - they can be like a dark shadow hovering over our lives. If your experiences have been full of any form of negativity for too long, this shadow can lurk over your shoulder like an invisible weight, whose leering presence you can't seem to get away from. No matter how hard you try, it seems to influence and impact every decision you choose to make for your life, and it takes on a whole life of its own. It has a voice and an opinion about everything you want to accomplish, and it dictates what you can and cannot do in your life.

PATHWAYS TO HEALING:
Overcoming Childhood Trauma and Adult Pain of Sibling Estrangement

This dark shadow represents a strong and unseen influence that distorts how you live your life; how you see the world, and how you fit into it. The despair makes you feel as though your life is not yours to live and, each day you wake up, you hope the shadow will dissipate and your past pain will just leave you alone.

Has this been your experience? Your past doesn't seem to leave you, particularly if it was filled with a lot of pain from those closest to you, and you have to wake up to its invisible face. It does whatever it wants in your life, and its presence steals your dreams and your future. It seems, no matter how hard you try to move forward in your life to make it better, you feel hopeless, angry and stuck. I want you to know there is a day in the future - I'm not sure how far ahead it is - when the shadow of that uninvited guest will be a distant memory.

Life is interesting, because it involves an arduous process of asking questions. We humans will always seek answers that help us understand life's numerous mysteries. We're always in a persistent frenzied search for meaning, something that provides an explanation to clear up our ignorance. We go on spiritual quests, we travel, we work harder, we try to accumulate wealth, depending on our circumstances… But what brings peace to the soul? The search for answers can take us down different paths.

When it comes to our emotional health and our search for

INTRODUCTION

meaning, there are many approaches we can take. I'd like to look at two of them: firstly, we will look internally and, based on our experiences, we make a decision and take responsibility for our life and grow or, secondly, we allow other people's expectations to define our lives for us. These two approaches are applied irrespective of what sort of emotional episode we are facing – whether it's love or dealing with the pains suffered from broken relationships. Unfortunately, when dealing with emotional difficulties, many people gravitate towards the latter option because, at some point in our upbringing, we have been conditioned to respond negatively and react to certain situations and family dynamics.

Dealing with emotional trauma can be challenging; this I know from experience. For many years, I was a victim of waves of emotional abuse for most of my life, so I can understand why it can be difficult for people to move on from these situations. For a long time, my life was on hold. I lived in a vicious cycle, going round and round in a maze of confusion without direction or purpose.

When you're under emotional distress, the easiest thing to do is to do everything that will prevent you from hurting again, and you stay stuck. Nevertheless, being easy doesn't equate to taking the right action because it isn't. In my opinion, dealing with emotional distress means taking the first steps towards reclaiming your life - working towards living and making decisions independent of the pain you feel. Without this, you'll remain trapped in the past, and the past will define your future.

Emotions are a part of our make-up as individuals. Without them, we're incomplete and, as much as we like to suppress them, everyone has an emotional reaction to everything. People might be skilled at hiding their expressions, but I think they have feelings about certain things - even when they don't show them. This can be seen as a trait of having passive-aggressive behaviour, because either they are stubborn and silently angry or they can't communicate their feelings. Society has branded emotions as a negative part of human behaviour that makes us seem weak, and so people tend to pander towards keeping their feelings to themselves, choosing instead to express and deal with their frustrations in other destructive ways—through alcohol, self-harm or domestic abuse. Nonetheless, the perceived weakness of expressing emotions by some doesn't mean we shouldn't show them - as long as we can support the emotions appropriately.

PREFACE

Having control over your emotions is an absolute necessity to living a balanced and fulfilled life. Sounds good, doesn't it? Having said that however, most times it can be impossible to do this because, unless you live in a cave all by yourself without any connection to other human beings and animals whatsoever, your emotions will always be influenced by external situations. *That* is why we can fall victim to abuse and maltreatment by others, which leaves us in a negative emotional state. In my experience, the effects of the emotional trauma I've gone through left me consumed by hurt, and made me feel like I had no control over my life. You can give too much power to this external entity that comes to torment you, and it can control your life for too long. However, when you take one hundred per cent responsibility for your life, you then start a trajectory of taking your control back. This way, you can make decisions independent of what you've gone through.

For example, you can have old pain—the sort that is buried deep in the subconscious—that is buried so deep even those who are the closest to us don't know about it. Such pain is carried in the darkest parts of our hearts, and only the carrier knows about it, and sometimes they don't even know how far their pain goes because it hurts too much to remember. So, when dealing with emotional turmoil, we start our healing from this dark place.

A particular passage from the Bible brought comfort to me during this period. Some of you may know it: the Book of Psalms 23:3$^{(NIV)}$ "...he refreshes my soul". I believe only God can see into the deepest parts of our soul, which hosts our will, mind and emotions, and therefore, only He can touch the deeper parts of my pain and guide me on my path to inner healing. This passage was crucial to my healing because of what I was going through. This helped me to face all the negativity I was experiencing and thinking, even when it was difficult to do so. At the time, the pain had become entirely too familiar, so much so that eliminating how it affected me seemed to be impossible. Only through God's intervention over time was I able to overcome my deepest pain. You will find that I refer to the Bible throughout this book, as several Scriptures helped me heal.

The effort required to reduce the pain that accompanies such situations can be difficult to apply, because dealing with old pain causes even more pain than the original suffering. Yet, I know everyone wants to be relieved of old pain, which is why going through a healing process is non-negotiable.

What I am asking you to consider here does have its consequences. You may find, as a result, that your current relationships will be affected, because you don't want to upset

PREFACE

others. By 'others' here, I refer to those who take advantage of your pain and mistreat you. You may call them bullies or insecure people, but you need not worry much about them now. If they need you, they know where to find you. If you don't already know, let me tell you that your pain empowers these people, and makes them feel good about themselves. Because your pain makes you vulnerable, it also gives them the leverage to manipulate and control you.

As soon as you decide to move away from your pain and towards a place of healing, a shift will occur, and things will start to change. The people who take advantage of you usually keep you in a box so that you'll remain their plaything. It may sound crude, but that's what they do. They will continue to control and manipulate you through your pain. At first, when you are in the thick of it, this will not be visible to you. However, when you look closely enough, you'll realise that this has always been the dynamics of your interaction with them. The reality of the matter is that there's also another pain in play here, and it's not just yours. This pain is those other people's insecurities and low self-esteem issues. Do you see, those who enjoy making other people feel miserable about themselves, do so because it helps them hide from their own pain and insecurities. The unfortunate thing about this is that both you and the other person(s) are not living as your genuine selves.

PATHWAYS TO HEALING:
Overcoming Childhood Trauma and Adult Pain of Sibling Estrangement

As human beings, we tend to identify with our past experiences. We forget that this only prevents us from being our genuine selves. The persons who have hurt you, also do not know, and haven't experienced the real you. We first need to know and release the real you, so you can be free. Perhaps you've hidden the truth about yourself because you never knew how to shine, so you protected yourself and your inner beauty. Releasing this will help you become one hundred per cent authentic! So, what's the truth about you? We're reminded in *Psalms 139:14* (NIV), which says: *"I praise You because I am fearfully and wonderfully made."*

We can make decisions for ourselves. We can. And when we do, things within and around us start to change. Every aspect of our life—from the moment we decide to stop living a life that continues to rotate in hurtful cycles—will begin to get better. So, if you're ready to become the real you, you can start your journey on the pathway to healing. To get on with living a full life, you will need to take a few steps in the right direction and change your location...

I assume you're reading this book because you've decided to heal the pain you've experienced. I congratulate you on this step, because now you've started your journey to be free from your past pain, and to embrace a brighter future.

CHAPTER ONE:
WHEN YOU THINK ABOUT IT

One way or another, we have all had experiences in our lives that have caused a great deal of pain. It's impossible to go through life without having bad experiences. This could have been anything from a parent's harsh treatment to never receiving the kind of love and affection we wanted and deserved. Life is a rollercoaster filled with ups and downs and, since we pray for only the positive stuff, bad things just happen. There's nothing anyone can do to get away from it—no matter their status.

Whenever one person has a connection with another person, bad things will happen. Many people have had experiences where their BFF (best friend forever) has ended up becoming their source of pain. This was supposed to be the one person they trusted and shared their dreams and aspirations with. So, anyone can be the cause of your pain. It does not matter if the person is a family member, a friend or a stranger. Everyone can be a source of pain to someone else; we are all human and can experience rejection from some of the most unlikely sources.

What was once a positive connection can, in even just one day, turn without warning. The love that once felt comforting, and served as a source of refuge, will morph into a cold and isolated place. You will no longer feel the love from them anymore and, just like that, they will turn away from you. There will be no STD (save the date) warnings. It will happen almost instantly, and it will look as though your life had just stood still whilst everything else around you was spinning out of control. We're told in Proverbs 27:5-6 [NIV]: *'Better is open rebuke than hidden love. Wounds from a friend can be trusted, but an enemy multiplies kisses.'*

It's good to know where we stand in relationships; have an awareness of the boundaries; protect each other, and interact from a place of trust, while mutually respecting one another. It is sad to say that, at times, your friend, a parent or sibling can be your enemy; this is nothing new.

A Pathway to Healing is my journey towards recovery from shame and rejection put upon me by some of the people who had cared for me since childhood. It is a story about the path I had to walk, which led me to a new place of accepting and embracing myself through self-love and inner healing. In the end, I came to believe there was a plan for me, even amidst the tragic storms that had taken over my life. I came to see that none of all I had gone through was a waste. Although it was the most severe emotional pain I had ever experienced in my life, it doesn't define me. I've come to understand that God loves me first, that He, Himself, is love, and that He accepts me just as I am. Therefore, I have grown to love and accept myself just as I am, through experiencing His unconditional love. This, in turn, has helped me to see myself and also love others.

As I've already mentioned, my story started at an early age, when I was a child. When I got older, I became more aware of what was happening to me, so I decided that I had to change midway through my story, and this has been a lifelong challenge for me. I grew up in a Caribbean family, where strict values and strong work ethics formed the foundations of my upbringing. You simply couldn't be feeble; it was taboo, as I'm sure some of you can identify with. Unconsciously, I was taught to believe that I would be loved and accepted only if I worked hard for it. Even with all my hard work, I still felt unloved by some. So let us look a bit deeper. Let's start with the nature of my dad's job. In those early years, he was away from home for long periods, and working in construction meant that sometimes we wouldn't see him for many weeks on end. Consequently, my mum was responsible for taking care of the home and the children.

Growing up in this environment took its toll on my childhood development. Aside from not getting much love from my father as a child, I also never knew where I fitted in. I always felt like the odd one out. This may have had something to do with being the last child of eight, but we didn't all grow up in the same house together. Even as a child, I was very emotionally aware, and I intuitively noticed other people's emotions. It was like a sixth sense, a superpower if you will. However, this didn't bring me great joy. My 'emotional superpowers' only encouraged others to rebuke and ridicule me throughout my formative years. Somehow, some of those I trusted used this against me. I felt as though they did not like me, and I was always mocked for being too sensitive whenever I commented or was upset about something. Some treated me differently—almost always in a negative, condemning way. I was always picked on as a child, bullied, and verbally and emotionally abused - repeatedly by some people.

THE BATTLE OF MY LIFE

So, in my own life, I experienced sibling rejection - at an age too young for any child to go through. One day, our lives changed—our home was already hostile and toxic, and I had to learn to grow up fast and fight a battle I did not know I would have to fight. I was not prepared, I was not equipped, and I was unsure and confused.

Why would a young child have to learn to survive in their own home? I did not know that this level of hostility, from people who were supposed to take care of me, would affect me later on in life. I had no understanding of the dynamics of adulthood, and that hurt people *hurt* other people. The bell kept on ringing for each new round in the boxing ring of my life, which lasted until I was much older.

So, over time, our home dynamics changed. I started to experience an increase in being bullied by a particular person who was becoming more intense. I was being spoken to more disrespectfully, blamed, shamed and accused of things I did not do. And, over the years, other people started to treat me in the same way. Since then, our lives have never been the same. Adjustment is a part of life, but when you end up having to fight a sibling at this level to survive, it takes its toll on your emotional health and well-being. It took a long time and, still, I think we never really did adjust fully.

I think, as the last child, I felt like the youngest one for sure. I felt safe with my mum, so I also felt I could tell her anything. So, there were times, as with any child, I would tell on my siblings if they did anything they shouldn't be doing, which I know leads to being picked on. Lol, I get it, but this was different. I started to feel like I was being treated differently by certain people. There was a certain level of disrespect that was directed towards me, which was fuelled with blame and anger. It seemed that if a conversation went on long enough, the insults would follow, or I was spoken more harshly to than others would be.

PATHWAYS TO HEALING:
Overcoming Childhood Trauma and Adult Pain of Sibling Estrangement

As you can imagine, being treated like this made me so sad, as this was not a normal sibling relationship. It was always filled with several accusations, belittling, and a lot of manipulation and control. This just wasn't normal.

Once I knew I could stand up for myself, there would be numerous arguments, which led to a lot of blame and shame, and verbal and emotional abuse, even though I did not know that's what it was at the time. So I experienced this cycle of toxicity throughout my teenage years, right through to adulthood.

You also know that things have gone wrong when other members of your family, and even people outside the family, start taking sides against you, not talking to you and, for some reason, treating you as the enemy.

I also unwind the story and life of Joseph in more detail, as I mentioned earlier. I can relate to him to some extent; he was also treated differently by some of his siblings; he knew what it was like to be picked on and to be enemy number one in his family.

1. Do you feel like that at all?

2. Can you relate to my story?

3. How does it make you feel?

"Yes," I hear you saying, *"So why didn't you ask why they were treating you like that?"* I mentioned that, over time, I started to see things unravelling. On several occasions, of course, I would ask the question of why I was being treated so aggressively and blamed for things I did not do. *"Why are you bullying me all the time?" "Why are you talking about me behind my back?" "Why do we always argue?"* I asked these questions over and over again. I would have understood if I had done something wrong and was told what it was, so that I could at least apologise and seek their forgiveness. But, there was nothing I had to ask forgiveness for, or that warranted this type of treatment. Not one time.

It was not until I reached my forties that I realised the life I thought was true was a lie. For many days, I had to process a lot of the emotional hurt I'd experienced. As I think about it now, I still can't believe I went through it. I would journal and write my poetry as a form of therapy for handling my feelings, although I did not know that's what I was doing at the time.

I have been more conscious of my surroundings, and glad that God has opened my eyes to a lot of the hidden things that have come out of the darkness into the light, from the past, the present and, I hope, for the future, but it has been so hard. Again, I have found many wise nuggets from the story of Joseph; it has a lot of character-building experiences that could not be ignored. Looking at all the things he went through in the first seventeen years of his life didn't seem to make sense, but it does if you look at the bigger picture, because God had a plan for each experience he went through. I had to believe that God had a plan for me too, and you need to believe that He also has a plan for you.

Anyone who has gone through this type of treatment will be able to relate to this. Maybe you've been in a situation where you felt misused or mistreated by those who were supposed to protect and care for you. Maybe it was a parent, sibling or family member. For me, the consequence of this harsh treatment had a lasting negative impact on my life. For most of my life, I grew up filled with fear, anger and uncertainty.

Maybe your experience was similar. But maybe it wasn't, and maybe your environment was more passive, where feelings were not expressed. Still, you always felt like the odd one out. You also felt like something within your family dynamics was missing, so this forced you to grow up quickly to survive, and you became a small adult—maturing faster than your peers. Our experiences make us become adults in children's bodies. Yet, while we still have child-like attributes and characteristics, our awareness of adult emotions and conversations become heightened.

I think it is explained so precisely in 1 Corinthians 13:11 [NIV]: *"When I was a child, I talked like a child, I thought like a child,*

WHEN YOU THINK ABOUT IT

I reasoned like a child. When I became a man, I put the ways of childhood behind me."

I've come to realise that traumatic experiences make it difficult to put away childish or childlike things or behaviour. This is because trauma has an unconscious effect on our emotions, and shapes our perception of the world around us. It affects our decision-making and even our relationships. The truth is that traumatic experiences can affect each of us differently.

For some people, their thinking will be stuck on the traumatic incident, and they will find it difficult to move on or get over it. A multitude of things can cause one to get stuck in life. Sometimes, we might seem to be doing so much, but in reality, we're not achieving anything meaningful. Well, I'm here to share with you that the fact you want to be healed from your childhood trauma or adult pain is enough to let you know that you can overcome anything, and that you are a fighter. Even though it seems like you've been knocked out and lost, you can get back up and gain more in the end.

With this mindset, if you keep moving forward, you will win and achieve great things. The experiences that happened years ago - or the ones that are happening now - can consume your life if you let them. Moving forward sometimes requires that you look back and see how far you've come. Doing this helps you to identify how much work you've done already. It motivates you to keep working towards your healing. It helps you realise that facing and dealing with the pain you've experienced is the best gift you can give yourself. I never felt that I was understood—nothing came easy for me, neither at school nor in my teen or adult years. Despite this, here I am, much older, with my first book and many more books to share.

If you do identify with not being understood, do you feel like you have to fight extra hard compared to others to achieve things in your life? Do you feel like nothing came easy for you? Maybe you have experienced hostility from some of your siblings. For whatever reason, some of them just never liked you. Or maybe, for years, you were bullied and abused verbally and emotionally, or even physically. Through all this, you did not understand the cause of the attack, pain and rejection. This left you feeling a great sense of indifference, shame, sadness, separation and exclusion from others. I want you to know it was not your fault!

If my story seems similar to what you went through, or you can identify with it in any way, know that you can pull through, just as I did. I think my experience has provided me with compassion for those who have gone through a similar thing. So I know and understand how you may be feeling. But you should know one thing: our emotions should not be the only parameters used to measure our lives. Even if they seem to be the only tangible thing we can rely on, our emotions will always be up one day and down another. You are a sum of many more parts than your emotions, making you bigger than your emotions. We are the sum of three parts: spirit, body and soul—our soul hosts our will, mind and emotions; our spirit hosts our wisdom, communion and conscience, and our body hosts our flesh, bone and blood. These aspects are mentioned throughout this book, in particular in Chapter Sixteen. However you may feel about your situation, I urge you to push through the barriers in your way, and find a safe place where you can find a breakthrough so you can break out.

When I thought I could take no more, and did not know what else to do, I reached my breakthrough moment. I just said again and again to God, "**HELP!** I can't do this anymore; I can't take this anymore; what do You want from me? Change my life." It may sound simple, but I had broken down to a point where I could no longer help myself. I needed a higher power to help me. I needed to know the truth about my situation, and I wanted to be set free. As soon as I called on God, things began to happen gradually. My situation started to change as the years flew by, and the truth about my life challenges started to unravel. I became aware that one of the reasons this was happening to me was due to the experiences others had had, which had caused them to be angry and disappointed with life. Unfortunately, I became the casualty of their pain because, whenever they expressed their negative emotion(s), they would direct it towards me. I found myself **fighting a battle** that had nothing to do with me! Has that been your experience? I'm also aware there is another battle we're fighting - a spiritual battle, which I talk about in **Chapter Eighteen**.

I hope that no matter how deep your pain is, you too will get to the point where you will start getting answers. I also hope that you'll start to feel a release and a change in your life, even if the situation around you hasn't changed in a long time. This will still make you feel better about yourself. The important thing in all of this is that you change, and change sometimes happens amidst the pain. You will feel more empowered to get up and take back control. Sometimes, our lives look normal until, one day, we realise that what we thought was normal was just a coping mechanism to deal with the pain inside us.

From childhood, we have been taught certain life principles. Most of us build our belief systems based on what we have heard and were taught in our families, or from the environment in which we grew up. As I've mentioned before, according to raisingchildren.net.au, our development is established between the ages of five and six, when the foundations are laid, which incorporate our character and personality, and morph us into the adults we later become. We take the 'teachings' into our adult lives, and these lead us to react to situations subconsciously, without even thinking whether how we perceive a situation is right or wrong. In the end, this brings us more pain—particularly if our reactions are not proportionate to the situation. For example, we may have triggers that make us overreact to a current situation, which will remind us of something we went through in the past that has not yet been dealt with.

You may be asking why this always happens to you. I think what we do by instinct, or unconsciously, is a true expression of what we believe internally about ourselves. For many of us, we may not realise that we live on a subconscious level. We may not know that the lessons we've learnt from childhood determine how we see and think about ourselves. They influence how we fit into the world, how we live our lives, what we believe about others, and also influence our expectations.

So, how do you identify with this cycle and pattern? It can show up in several ways. For instance:

- The inappropriate behaviour towards or mistreatment by others when you interact with them – and it becomes a normal way of interacting, and you don't even realise that you should be treated better.
- Being spoken to in a negative or derogatory way by others, with no apologies.
- Feeling uncomfortable around certain people, and you just feel something is 'not right'.
- Being left out of social gatherings or celebrations.

- Being shamed in front of others or in private.

- Being love-bombed, by receiving gifts, to do something you don't want to.

- Over-the-top attention, in exchange for doing things for others.

- Gas-lighting is a form of psychological abuse, where a person or group makes someone question their sanity, perception of reality, or memories.

- Manipulation and control – emotional abuse used by someone to get their own way.

- Disregard – to pay no attention, to treat as unworthy of regard or notice.

- Triangulation – a form of manipulation in which one person will not communicate directly with another person. Instead, they use a third person to communicate on their behalf, forming a triangle. The aim is to divide and conquer.

- Being separated from other family members, or people of positive influences.

So, I'm not a doctor or psychologist, but I have come to understand - through my research and what I went through - that this list above is not exhaustive and, sadly, it can identify an individual who has a personality disorder associated with being narcissistic. I am not giving a diagnosis of anyone's character or emotional state; rethink.org explains it as follows:

- Narcissistic personality disorder can mean you have a high sense of self-importance.

- They may fantasise about unlimited success and want attention and admiration.

- They may feel they are more entitled to things than other people are

- They may act selfishly to gain success.

- They may be unwilling or unable to acknowledge the feelings or needs of others.

Maybe we're in an era now, where these characteristics are more evident in our relationships and society, as we're all part of the human race. I know, for me, this is what I experienced — and so much more. Imagine, this 'characteristic' or, I would like to also add, this 'spiritual influence' was embodied in different individuals throughout my life. We're told in the Bible that the enemy of our soul wants to steal, kill and destroy us, but God wants to give us life (read John 10:10 [NIV]). I now know that the other people intended to hurt me very deeply, and this makes me feel so sad!

Over the years, as I was going through my relationship challenges, and in an attempt to find answers, I came across

PATHWAYS TO HEALING:
Overcoming Childhood Trauma and Adult Pain of Sibling Estrangement

several psychologists and doctors. I finally found some resources and information I needed to help me understand, and walk through the emotional minefield, and the cause for it. You may find them useful resources. As a disclaimer, I am not affiliated with these individuals or their organisations, but I know you will find their information helpful:

1. **Dr Ramani Durvasula** is a renowned licensed clinical psychologist, who is one of the best-selling authors, who teaches on all things narcissistic.

2. **Psych2Go** make creative content around the areas of mental health and psychology that's created to entertain and educate.

3. **Dr Henry Cloud** is an acclaimed leadership expert, psychologist and best-selling author. He helps people to create healthy boundaries in their relationships, among other things.

4. **Beverly Engel** is an internationally recognised psychotherapist and an author, who is an acclaimed advocate for victims of sexual, physical and emotional abuse. Her information helped me a lot when I started on my journey.

Being treated like this can lead to you living life with a negative mindset. It can cause you to develop negative thoughts, habits, patterns and reactions, which reproduce the same experiences daily. This creates a feeling of disappointment, which will make you wonder why your life hasn't changed yet. You start questioning your entire life, wondering why you are still in the same place.

I've stated previously that we all have misplaced emotions. We act based on what we have experienced, on what we were taught, and how we were treated from early childhood. Our childhood experiences came about to influence our character in ways we couldn't even understand.

This subconscious programming forms our character, our way of thinking, habits and how we perceive the people and situations around us. This programming seeps into our decision-making process when it comes to trying to achieve what we want in our lives. We're more than our physical selves. We are spiritual and 'soulish' beings. Issues arise when we focus on just one area alone. While this is not all bad, what happens is that we forget to identify with the rest of the elements that make up our core personality, which I've stated is our spirit, body and soul. These three entities form the basis of what makes us human, enabling us to connect and communicate with God.

If these elements are taken out of the equation, it can create an imbalance, and this can lead to feeling incomplete and empty. What we should strive towards is oneness with our soul and spirit. This should be everyone's desire, because we can then start living from a place of wholeness, which is what everyone wants.

CHAPTER TWO:
FAMILY FEUDS HAS ROOTS

Having a family is a beautiful thing. It is probably one of the most beautiful things an individual can have. A family is like a backbone, because they support and show us love when things begin to get tough. Having a good family is a very special feeling. However, bad things can happen within the family dynamics. Some families are dysfunctional, and therefore family members might feel different levels of pain. This causes a lot of stress for the people in the family, and this can go on for years.

Our family is the place where we have our first introduction to relationships. However your family looks, or however many people it's made up of, it shapes our self-worth and identity through the positive and negative interactions we have, like love, discipline and the boundaries we have experienced with our parents (or caregivers), siblings and extended family members. How we relate to our immediate family influences the relationships we have later in life. The training ground for relationships is taught within our families. Each family is built on a generational foundation, which influences the way individuals do certain things and what they believe is

PATHWAYS TO HEALING:
Overcoming Childhood Trauma and Adult Pain of Sibling Estrangement

right or wrong. It shows up in how we are interacting; how we speak to each other; how we love and protect each other; how we are taught or not taught, and how we deal with conflict. How we deal with anger influences us, and we then start to make our second connections which are with society. Therefore, whatever we've gone through shapes our view and every aspect of our lives. That is why having a good family unit is very important to everybody's upbringing.

However, no matter how perfect a family is, there are occasional fallouts. Despite all the love and goodwill that exists within a family, fights happen, disagreements and hurtful moments take place, and sometimes, they are left unresolved. Therefore, this is very normal. Moreover, whenever this happens, it can be quickly and easily resolved in a way in which everyone can be satisfied.

A family is a place where everyone should show love and admiration for each other, irrespective of the situation. But, as it is with everything, sometimes the opposite happens. For example, it can be that some family members are mistreating you. For whatever reason, they don't like you and they make this known whenever you're around. So, what do you do then? What do you do when how you're treated by those closest to you hurts you all the time? We all need a place to belong—to identify with as our place of safety. This is what helps to shape us; it forms us and makes us into who we are.

FAMILY FEUDS HAS ROOTS

When family members hurt us like this, the pain cuts deep — so deep because, at first, we don't recognise what is happening. As I stated before, even though you don't feel comfortable with it, you believe it to be normal, seeing as no one has challenged the behaviour or talked about it as a problem. What is happening hurts you, but you think that's how it should be. You've had no experience that tells you otherwise, so you continue to wallow in this misery. However, as time goes by, the pain keeps getting deeper and it warps your mind. It distorts and shapes us with a negative perception, and influences how we behave. We wouldn't even know this because we've lived like this for so long that it has become normal. This pain goes directly to the core of our existence.

I have discovered that dealing with this pain requires you to find answers and be honest with yourself. There is no way around this. It's either this, or you let the pain continue to destroy you. When we don't confront this feeling head on, we remain vulnerable and accustomed to unhealthy behaviour towards us, even from other people outside our family as well. We become puppets to be used and dumped on by anyone who feels like it. This is not good.

We can see ourselves as victims, which I can understand, and so will other people who are looking for victims. They will find you and treat you as you think you are. Did you hear me? I'll say it again: as you think you are! I don't say this to blame you, but to impress upon you that you have to change your mindset towards yourself and increase your energy levels.

Your pain will attract negative people. Equally, your positive energy attracts positive people. So some adjustments need to be made to change your mindset from being a victim to a victor, and to start believing it and acting like it, and this takes time. I love the following Scripture, which is full of compassion and love:

Ezekiel 16:4-6 (NIV) – *"4 On the day you were born your cord was not cut, nor were you washed with water to make you clean, nor were you rubbed with salt or wrapped in cloths. 5 No one looked on you with pity or had compassion enough to do any of these things for you. Rather, you were thrown out into the open field, for on the day you were born you were despised. 6 Then I passed by and saw you kicking about in your blood, and as you lay there in your blood I said to you, 'Live!'"*

God speaks life over every area of your existence—where you've felt naked, exposed or uncovered. Parents try their best to nurture their children. But, on some occasions, there can be one or two that slip through the net of LOVE. They are viewed as a troubled child; the one that is too wise; the one who has too much to say; the one with power over their lives… Because of this, they are ignored, ostracised and rejected. Some families do have deep-rooted secrets that lurk in the depths of the cut umbilical cords, that fed us in the

FAMILY FEUDS HAS ROOTS

womb of our generational bloodline. These iniquities can manifest from generation to generation.

In these situations and cycles of certain behaviours, you'll see similar happenings and experiences. For example, it could be that all the men in your family are unable to commit to a relationship, or the women are dominant and controlling. It can be anything that runs through the bloodline. Similar things might happen in your family, intensifying the pain which they inflict on you. These deep-rooted secrets cause fractured relationships within individual families. They affect extended families, as well. And this will continue to be a problem, because no one has dealt with it until, one day, someone gets the revelation that this has been going on for far too long, and decides that **enough is enough**! So, could that person be **YOU**?

So let's unpack the 'Family Feuds have roots'. Sibling **rejection** and **estrangement** are nothing new in the Bible. The first sibling dispute happened between two brothers; you may have heard of them: Cain and Abel, the sons of Adam and Eve, who set a precedent for all other sibling relationships that followed. Jealousy and envy overtook Cain, and caused him to kill his brother. He then lied about the murder to God! Can you believe that? As though God didn't see what he did? Jealousy will always make you lie: first to yourself and then to God and others. As a result, God cursed Cain and marked him for life.

PATHWAYS TO HEALING:
Overcoming Childhood Trauma and Adult Pain of Sibling Estrangement

Sibling disagreements and estrangements show up in many families in the Bible, and maybe you see a pattern in your own family. Cain was a farmer, and his sacrifice to God was a portion of his crops. One day, he learned that God was more pleased with Abel's sacrifice. Abel was a herdsman, so his sacrifices to God consisted of the fattest portion of his flock. Enraged with jealousy, Cain killed his brother. Consequently, because of the brutal way Abel died, God cursed the earth and Cain was unable to farm the land. Cain was cursed by God, and became a fugitive and wanderer. In some commentaries, it states that Cain's offering was rejected because it was not a blood sacrifice, or that Cain replicated what his mother and father had done when they sinned.

He offered God his fruit of the ground, just like his parents, Adam and Eve, who covered themselves with fig leaves. All Cain had to do was give God the same offering as Abel had done—it was all about obedience. He could have changed his mind and offered to God what would have been acceptable. Instead, rather than honouring God, he made his brother the focus of his rejection. He took out his frustrations on his brother, Abel, by taking his life.

This story of Cain and Abel shows how the feeling of rejection can make us do unpalatable things if we don't handle our jealousy properly. Cain took his brother's life, and nothing is worse than taking someone's life. It shows us that rejection can eat away at our souls and make us do inhumane things.

FAMILY FEUDS HAS ROOTS

So, if you've had clashes with your siblings, then that's where healing needs to take place. We might decide to continue living our lives the way things have always been, because facing the truth about what is confronting us is difficult. I know and I understand this feeling. I'm one of you. I've been there. But you must understand that while living in this kind of denial is beneficial to you now, it is nothing compared to how you'll feel after you deal with your issues. You just need to be brave, get external support if needed, and take a stance and say, "Hey, let's deal with this and see if we can get back to the place of LOVE." It's always hard to go against the tide of family dynamics, but we all deserve to be free from what truly pains us. It can be challenging, because the family might accept they need to deal with the issues or might not want to. This Scripture describes it well:

Proverbs 18:19-20 (NIV) *"A brother wronged is more unyielding than a fortified city; disputes are like the barred gates of a citadel."*

So let's now look at Joseph's story. Let's take a brief look at the family dynamics he came from, and where the sons of Jacob learned the type of behaviour of rejection and betrayal. In biblical times, polygamy was a part of their culture; I can't explain it, so I won't even try. Men could have many wives, and Jacob had four. So Joseph's parents, Jacob and Rebekah, had him and his brother, Benjamin. Jacob had a twin brother called Esau. Being twins, it was recorded that they even

PATHWAYS TO HEALING:
Overcoming Childhood Trauma and Adult Pain of Sibling Estrangement

fought in the womb! So even at their unborn stage, they were fighting! There's so much there, it would take too long to unpack. And now the same behaviour was showing up in his children! What a revelation *(drop the mic)*. So, we pick up the story where the two brothers, Jacob and Esau (who was the oldest), became estranged from each other over the family inheritance. I know it's a lot; stay with me. You can read the full story in Genesis 25:19-34$^{(NIV)}$, but this is a concise view of their story:

...One day Esau came in from hunting, he was very tired and hungry. He was so overcome with hunger that he lost all logic! So he did something strange: he ended up selling his birthright to Jacob for a bowl of Caribbean soup... Now, if you've ever tasted this soup, you can understand why he did it.

With all the pieces of goodness that make it the best soup... imagine with me for a while... You have to add the following ingredients: a few pieces of cooked chicken, stew beef or pigs tail (yes, you heard right, some people do eat this). (You only choose one meat at a time for this dish.) You add your sweet potato, your white or yellow yam, your green banana, your kneaded dumplings, your seasoning — thyme, scallion, black pepper, salt to taste — carrots, plus the added cock soup (with the small noodles). Start cooking it in the morning for about 2-3 hours. So, by the time you finish your housework and finish your food shopping, the soup will be ready!!!

FAMILY FEUDS HAS ROOTS

It's the kind of soup that will just make you find one spot or corner to enjoy it without being disturbed. Lol…. I'm joking. I'm back in the room now! I'm sure Jacob's soup was not a Caribbean dish; it was lentil soup. … but I can understand that if it were, you could be persuaded to sell *anything* in exchange for a bowl. So seriously, this sounds crazy to me, but he did it. Afterwards, when Isaac their father had grown very old, he sent Esau one day to get some of his favourite meat, saying that when he returned he should have his father's blessing.

But Rebekah heard this, and determined that Jacob should have the blessing instead. So she prepared meat, then dressed Jacob in some of his brother's clothing, covering his hands and neck with the skin of a goat, and sent him to his father, and Isaac blessed him, for his sight was dim, and he thought it was Esau.

When Esau returned, he was very angry with Jacob, and Isaac was deeply grieved to think he had been deceived, but he blessed Esau as well, who became prosperous and had large possessions and great power.

After this, Jacob went to his mother's people, where he met Rachel, whom he loved very dearly. He told Laban, her father, that he would serve him faithfully for seven years if Rachel might be his wife, and Laban consented to this. At the end of the seven years, however, he cheated Jacob out of marrying

Rachel, and said he had to first marry Leah, as she was the older sister, but if he would serve *another* seven years he might have Rachel also. So Jacob served another seven years for Rachel, and then they were married.

Later Esau and Jacob met, and were very glad to see each other, for Jacob had repented of what he had done, and God had forgiven him, and Esau forgave him also. So this is where the generational family feuds continued through the bloodline down to Joseph and his siblings: Jacob showed more favouritism towards him than his other siblings, and this resulted in his brothers' envy, stemming from that perceived favouritism. It's sad to learn that people's thoughts and feelings towards you do not always match up with the way they interact with you. A person can claim to love you, only for you to find out that they actually hate you. Hidden hate doesn't just happen; it starts small, grows, and manifests into different levels of hate, and its roots go deep because it started from a place of bitterness, envy and jealousy. I discuss this more in Chapter Ten.

If you were the least favoured child, you would know how you've been treated, and how this has made you feel as a result. It is time to change your mind about how you see yourself. So, let's do the first set of action steps to identify the aspects of your life that have been affected by your parents' or siblings' maltreatment, or from other people, which may include some of the five areas I will refer to throughout this book:

1. **Physical abuse** – The intention or act of causing injury or trauma.

2. **Spiritual abuse** – Any attempt to exert power and control over someone using religion, faith or beliefs.

3. **Sexual** - Experience of being molested, abusive sexual behaviour.

4. **Emotional abuse** – Yelling at you, verbally insulting you, swearing at you, or making you feel rejected.

5. **Neglect** – Suffering from a lack of proper care (be it shelter, food or emotional support).

ACTION STEPS

What is your Sibling Rejection Story?

1. What are the things that you have experienced?

   _____
   _____
   _____
   _____

2. Where does it hurt?

   _____
   _____
   _____
   _____

3. What treatments from your sibling(s) are you still tolerating?

   _____
   _____
   _____
   _____

4. How did your parents treat you differently from your sibling(s)? How did it make you feel?

   _____
   _____
   _____
   _____

FAMILY FEUDS HAS ROOTS

5. What are the things you push to the back of your mind because they hurt too much (If you can't deal with it right now, leave this question out)?

   _____
   _____
   _____
   _____

6. What kind of life do you want to experience?

   _____
   _____
   _____
   _____

7. What do you like about yourself?

   _____
   _____
   _____
   _____

PATHWAYS TO HEALING:
Overcoming Childhood Trauma and Adult Pain of Sibling Estrangement

CHAPTER THREE:
CHILDHOOD TRAUMA AND ADULT PAIN

Sibling rejection is not an easy issue to look at or to talk about but, to be honest, we've all experienced it in some shape or form. It can be one of the most challenging experiences, full of confusion, humiliation, secret jealousy and pain. This forces you to question everything you believe to be your truth. Why do those closest to me want to hurt me? Why would those who should know me better than anyone else want to treat me like a stranger? These questions can be insurmountable. Getting your control back doesn't come from others but from an internal instinct to seek change in your life, and a desire for a change in your relationships and circumstances. For the sake of providing perspective, I'd like to provide you with a definition of what power means. According to the Oxford Dictionary, POWER refers to:

- The ability or capacity to do something. Synonyms of power include ability, capacity, capability, potential and competence.

- The capacity or ability to direct or influence the behaviour of others or the course of events.

PATHWAYS TO HEALING:
Overcoming Childhood Trauma and Adult Pain of Sibling Estrangement

- A physical strength and force exerted by something or someone on another entity.

- The supply of a device with mechanical or electrical energy.

- When something moves or travels with great speed or force.

From the above definitions, and coupled with the topics we've been discussing, you can see how pertinent it is for you to have the power to control your life within your grasp. If not, you expose yourself to the influence of others and the influence of external forces. When your power resides within you, the trajectory and path your life takes are within your control. As I talk about losing your power, you might think one relinquishes their power because of other people, but no. Many other things, aside from human beings, might hold the power to control your life. One of them is the pain and hurt you've experienced in your life. If you stay stuck on them, they control your decisions and everything else in your life. I emphasised this in the previous chapter, so I'm certain, by now, that you understand how pain and hurt can affect you.

This is why I'm writing this book: I hope to help you get your strength and be empowered to live life on *your* terms. It doesn't matter where or when power was taken from you, and I don't negate what you've experienced. My aim is to give you some of the wisdom I've learnt, and how getting my voice back empowered me through my healing. In the end, you'll begin to feel that you have the right to feel good about yourself, and that you have the right to live a better and fuller life. As the Bible says, *"Those who sow with tears will reap with songs of joy"* – Psalms 126:5 (NIV). This is what I wish to help you achieve with this book.

No one hopes to live a challenging life. Irrespective of how life is, everyone wants to live and enjoy it to the full. Nevertheless, sometimes life just happens and things don't go as planned. It is normal—it happens. Physical sickness, a broken heart and spirit, a lost relationship, happiness, hope, and dreams are all part of life. But what happens after we encounter these experiences is usually our greatest undoing as human beings.

When confronted with any difficulty, we buckle and retract. We change and become timid. It's hard to keep going sometimes; we're meant to defeat whatever challenges we face, or else they will defeat us. Instead of facing the situation head-on, we create fantasies in our heads to prevent us from facing the reality of our situation. This is both ineffective and counterproductive to our healing process. If healing is to take place in our lives, the first step is to admit the hurt. It may sound like an obvious observation, but many people don't do this. People become so familiar with the pain that they forget how life was without it. This makes them forget there is a place of healing. Is it surprising that this happens? So, someone who doesn't face their problem can't admit they have one. Why would they find a solution to something that doesn't exist?

But if you have been there, if you've experienced any sort of pain, you'll understand why people do this. I must admit, pain is a very uncomfortable experience that is hard to deal with. So, instead of facing their problems, many people just wish them away. They say to themselves it's not real, because finding an end to the pain is as difficult as dealing with the source of the pain itself.

You don't have to live like that. There is an end to the pain. There is an end to that which is tearing your heart apart. We tend to say it is well with my soul, but we also need to remember that our hearts need to be mended as well. We can't walk around with a broken heart and not wonder: is this the life I'm meant to live? When will my heart be mended? When will I be happy? Don't let the pain you're experiencing push you to forget what God says. If you don't know it, He promises to do this for you and me: *"He heals the brokenhearted and binds up their wounds"*– Psalms 147:3 *(NIV)*.

If admitting that you're in pain is difficult, you might ask why you should do it. Why should I increase my pain by admitting that I am in pain, when it's much easier creating fantasies that numb me against feeling that pain? For one, fantasies don't make the pain go away, and they sure don't make you feel any less pained. Even if they do, you begin to live an unproductive and ineffective life. Once you admit that there's some hurt you're carrying in your soul, you can then start on the path to solving the problem. The thing is that we carry around our emotions like a piece of baggage. Whether we like it or not, avoiding our feelings doesn't mean that these emotions are less impactful in our lives.

If anything, it just makes us feel unskillful, because this baggage affects us. The baggage we carry affects our physiological and psychological states. I discuss in more detail the emotional Weights and Baggage we carry in Chapter Nineteen. These distressing feelings come in different forms and affect us in unimaginable ways. If we don't deal with what is affecting us, we'll hurt ourselves and the people around us. Think of it like this: imagine you had a faulty car. Let's assume the car has a faulty brake system. If you don't attend to this fault, will it go away? Better still, if you don't attend to it, does it mean the car's braking system is not faulty, even when it is? You can use your answers to these questions to evaluate your reaction to emotional distress.

I've talked about how your emotional imbalances affect you. Here are a few physical symptoms that could be a result of what you've gone through; you'll notice when you're carrying a lot of issues in your mind. They're confirmed as physical evidence of the stress in our body; I don't claim to diagnose anyone's symptoms.

- Increase in blood pressure.

- High hormone secretion—beyond the normal limits. This is visible in our behaviour.

- We become easily sensitive and highly irritable.

- We isolate ourselves from others, so that we don't have to talk about our problems or stress.

- Our breathing rate increases.

There is an epidemic caused by stress and depression that we need to face and deal with. Wherever the stress is coming from, we need to give ourselves time to think clearly and find help. You can do this by taking time out to relax. You can relax by going for a walk, taking up new hobbies, or meeting new people in a relaxed environment. Also, you can learn to make and maintain a schedule. Living a scheduled life is the key to a balanced life. If you are not well, and you're not taking care of yourself, how can you help others? The power is in taking some time for you. This may mean creating time in your diary for you to do nothing; go out for lunch by yourself; visit the park or the beach, or just reconnect with your inner self and recharge. I provide some more fun, holistic and practical tools that you can implement into your life in **Chapter Twenty-Seven - Pathways to Healing.**

It's important to remember that the time you take out for yourself will empower you, help you to focus on your goals, and enable you to let go of the things that no longer serve you. Letting go of things or people takes time, and will have an impact on your new decision-making process. But, if it's a relationship that is hurting you, a decision must be made to ensure you are now treated with respect, and that means firstly respecting yourself again.

PATHWAYS TO HEALING:
Overcoming Childhood Trauma and Adult Pain of Sibling Estrangement

CHAPTER FOUR:
THE R-WORD – REJECTION

Rejection, no matter how we see it, is one of the most hurtful feelings anyone can ever contend with. Unfortunately, this is one thing every man, woman, boy and girl has had to deal with at some point in their lives. Whether it is being overlooked for a sporting event at school as a child, or being denied a promotion at work, rejection happens often and in any kind of situation. Nonetheless, whatever the reason for rejection, it doesn't make it any less painful.

Rejection damages the soul, which can lead to the destruction of our will. This affects our mind and, ultimately, our sense of belonging. The feeling of rejection leads to a feeling that goes straight to the roots of our being, and no one should have to go through that. It brings a hurt that seems to capture prisoners no matter who they are, taking us into the deepest and darkest places of our souls. It eats away at our mental stability and brings about confusion. Rejection makes us ask questions: What did I do to deserve this? Why don't I feel like I belong? Why do I feel so lost? What's wrong with me? It opens up thoughts of blame and shame, which I talk about more in **Chapter Seven**. Rejection tries to replace your love with hate and to break your heart into many pieces.

Despite this horrible situation, however, you need to look inwardly and ask yourself whether you have allowed the situation to define you. Have you allowed it to alter your personality? Have you become a shadow of your former self?

To understand the pain that is experienced after being rejected, it is important to point out that it is expressed in many different forms, e.g., being turned down, dismissed, abandoned, forsaken, deserted, shut out, excluded, avoided, ostracised, being given the cold shoulder, and in many other forms.

You may think the feeling of rejection happens in isolation, but it doesn't. Rejection brings other forms of negativity that pollute and torment the mind — guilt, shame and isolation — making the whole situation worse than it should be. Rejection is an emotion that unsettles our deepest desires to feel safe, to be loved, and to belong. In the face of this challenge, we ask ourselves the following questions:

- Who am I?

- Where do I belong?

- Who loves me unconditionally?

THE R-WORD - REJECTION

- What is my purpose?

We all have a journey to walk through in this life and, at times, it does include a balance of joys and pains. While it may not be obvious to you now, your entire life was mapped out before you were born. God is good, and He never neglects us. If He took His time to create and breathe life into you, He surely has a good plan for you. He does not make bad things happen to us; bad things happen for a lot of reasons. And because we live in a broken world that has broken people who, from time to time, hurt each other, bad and good things will always happen in tandem. The psalmist declares:

"⁴⁵ My frame was not hidden from You when I was made in the secret place; when I was woven together in the depths of the earth. ¹⁶ Your eyes saw my unformed body; all the days ordained for me were written in Your book before one of them came to be." – Psalms 139:15-16 (NIV)

Rejection brings about a pain that does not care about you. It is out to make you suffer psychologically, spiritually and physically at the highest level. One of our greatest fears is the fear of being abandoned. That is what rejection brings. It brings you face to face with a taskmaster whose only intention is to make you its prisoner. By making you feel alone, it preys on your sense of not feeling loved and accepted. This way, it brings about the kind of excruciating pain that makes even the strongest person tremble.

PATHWAYS TO HEALING:
Overcoming Childhood Trauma and Adult Pain of Sibling Estrangement

Rejection is a negative spirit or entity, whose sole purpose is to separate you from others. Fear in itself is a spirit, and it manifests itself when you have to do something outside your comfort zone. By restricting your sense of adventure, the spirit of fear is negative and it wants to keep you in a box. It prevents you from exploring new areas of life, thereby keeping you compliant. So fear empowers rejection by making you feel alone and isolating you from others. It keeps you away from your group of friends and family, preventing you from connecting with other people for fear of rejection, and so the cycle begins.

God made all of us for love. But to love another requires that someone else is in the equation. That may be other people who are in your life right now. Be encouraged by Deuteronomy 31:6 (NIV) - *"Be strong and courageous. Do not be afraid or terrified because of them, for the Lord your God goes with you; He will never leave you nor forsake you."* The last part of this passage emphasises God's promise never to neglect anyone. This means He will never depart from you. This passage is every kind of assurance you need to keep going on this quest for healing. He has said He is with you every step of the way; God will not let you out of His sight; He knows where you are, even in your pain. Do you know that God didn't send His Son to redeem the pure at heart—He sent His Son to save people like you and me. He is especially interested in people struggling in life. So, as you continue to find healing, know that God will never neglect you. And, even after you have healed, He will still be there to guide and protect you.

Emotional pain, as we know it, is a feeling that resides in the deepest part of our souls. It is a parasite and, like every parasite, it consumes from within. The effect of emotional pain is so severe it affects both our physiological and mental health. (I covered this in the previous chapter).

At times, the pain is so deep that we can't express how we feel in words. Sometimes, it is almost unreal, and has us thinking if this is truly our reality. We begin to ask if we are the only ones experiencing this sort of pain. With this line of thinking, isolation and loneliness begin to build up. In the book of Genesis, God said it is not good for man to be alone. Although the passage uses the gender-specific noun, man, God was referring to human beings in general. According to the story of creation, we are a mirror image of God, and He created us in His image and likeness. In retrospect, He created us to be in a relationship with Him first, and then with others, to feel, respond, think and find a solution to problems, and experience joy and happiness. The most important attribute God gave us is the ability to interact with God Himself and with one another. This attribute is crucial to our growth as individuals.

Without human relationships, the human race — and civilisation as we know it — will become extinct. From the onset, our ability to live together in units has been crucial to our survival. It has allowed us to protect ourselves, and enabled the creation of customs and traditions that regulate our interactions. As a result, we have a balanced and healthy relationship with one another. It has promoted the spirit of fellowship and kinship that fosters belonging. In the book of Genesis, something entered into the perfect Garden of Eden that produced a pandemic into the hearts and souls of the human race. Its effect would touch everyone born into the world, and that is pain.

The Oxford English Dictionary Online describes **PAIN** as 'a highly unpleasant physical sensation caused by illness or injury.' It goes further to give other meanings to the word, including: suffering, agony, affliction, torture, torment, discomfort, mental suffering or distress, sorrow, grief, heartache, heartbreak, sadness, unhappiness, distress, desolation, misery, wretchedness, despair, desperation, emotional suffering and trauma.

Pain comes in different forms. I am sure you can identify with one or more of the synonyms above. People can live their lives, year after year, in a perpetual state of pain. The unnerving part is that they won't even know it. This sort of pain is so deep and hidden that it has become a part of them. As a result, they have become immune to its existence. It is so serious that, sometimes, close relatives won't even know about their pain. Then one day, the truth is revealed, and they realise they have been living in a negative state of mind. For someone in this state, this can be a very big revelation—a massive awakening!

I know this will sound strange to you. If I were you, I'd be surprised as well. How can anyone feel pain and not know they are in pain? One thing to consider is that we are creatures of habit. If we've lived in an environment where we don't feel loved, and then we experience one that is completely different—one where we are showered with love—our emotions are thrown into a tailspin. We begin to draw comparisons between our previous experiences and the new reality that has presented itself. This is when you start to understand that your past experiences were neither good nor healthy. The revelation of how you've been living in pain all this time is huge, because you didn't know the situation you were living under wasn't normal. You had become accustomed to it.

To prevent blame in such an abusive relationship—the one where you were not shown enough love—you start to shut down. You grow immune to yourself and your reality, because it hurts so much. This leads you to live a life of seclusion, to protect yourself from abuse and the lack of love and honour. I mentioned in **Chapter Two** that Cain had a curse over his life because he refused to honour God with his offering. I think honour is a significant word, so I will be unpacking this in the next chapter.

PATHWAYS TO HEALING:
Overcoming Childhood Trauma and Adult Pain of Sibling Estrangement

CHAPTER FIVE:
HONOUR

Honour means 'to hold in high esteem'. It also means 'to admire, respect, protect and be an influencer'.

Most people who have experienced rejection in its deepest form do not feel honoured. They do not feel respected and, of course, they feel unprotected. So, until you start to learn to honour, respect and protect yourself first, you will continue to validate the pain. It will continue to define you until you do something about it.

If you've been told something consistently, such as you're stupid, you're too sensitive, your opinion does not matter, or if you've been made to feel irrelevant for a long time, you will begin to accept it as your truth. Eventually, you become conditioned to this situation, and you begin to respond to it as your new norm. This is true if you have lived like this for the majority of your life. It is more telling if you've gone through something like this from a young age, because you are susceptible to everything and vulnerable to the ways of the world. At your young age, you're not capable of comprehending the difference between right and wrong. What happens is that we become numb and don't even realise it, because we think this is the norm.

PATHWAYS TO HEALING:
Overcoming Childhood Trauma and Adult Pain of Sibling Estrangement

We can become accustomed to disorder and pain in our lives, if we're in a situation where the people around us don't show us unconditional love, or there are no healthy boundaries in place. This can also happen when we feel that people don't accept us for some reason. Situations like this bring about an uncomfortable feeling, and you begin to get the sense that something isn't right. You start to feel like invisible barriers are preventing you from attaining deep and meaningful relationships and preventing progression in life in general.

There can also be unspoken pain or hurt that you keep receiving from people within your social circles, making you wonder why you're always getting treated this way. We can live our lives feeling there is something out of place in our relationships. We question why we are experiencing a pattern where we feel something is not right. This can hinder and prevent us from moving into greater relationships. It can keep you from enjoying your life, and prevent you from feeling good about yourself.

We all have a story, and this is mine. I hope it will help you understand that you can reclaim your life from those who caused you pain, or from what you have experienced or are currently experiencing. I want my story to show you that you can use the pain you've experienced as fuel to be empowered, and gain the strength to help you from within. In overcoming your pain, I want you to believe in yourself again, love yourself, and know you can overcome anything.

This means you start to take back control of your own life. This is not to be used to enact revenge towards those who have hurt you. It is a state you use to nurture and become the precious diamond you are meant to be.

During my experience, I was able to get back up, even though I wasn't expecting anything to change for a few reasons. I was sceptical about it, because I didn't believe that getting back up would stop the pain. Irrespective of this, here I stand today, despite the challenging life experiences I have gone through. I have come to learn that my life is to be lived and enjoyed. And while so much of it was used fighting one battle or another, it was not wasted! So, what do you do when you go through so many ups and downs in life, and you don't know when things will change?

Life has its seasons—just like the natural seasons of time. As we experience these different seasons of life that bring their challenges, we need to learn to adapt to them. We have got to live and keep moving forward. This is important so that, one day, we will thrive again, regardless of the season of life that we are in.

If you can keep this up, and identify with a renewed purpose, you will birth something new within you, and then you will begin to identify with the strength that is within you. It isn't until the stretching starts that we are aware growth is required in our character. I talk about 'Seeing Through the Eyes of

PATHWAYS TO HEALING:
Overcoming Childhood Trauma and Adult Pain of Sibling Estrangement

Purpose' in **Chapter Fifteen**. It's only then that something new will come forth from new experiences. These new experiences have to emerge from us, requiring us to move away from the place we are familiar with.

By uprooting old hurts and the burden of new relationship challenges, changes will begin to happen right before your eyes. It's only making space for the new things that are yours to enjoy. The new experiences available to you begin to bear fruit in your life! The new opportunities start presenting themselves to areas of your life you never thought possible, but this doesn't come without some work. Everything great and worthwhile is accompanied by some form of pressure and, at times, it seems too much, but it is used to birth something new in your life, which you can use to help others if you want to.

CHAPTER SIX:
TAG, YOU ARE NEXT

Reflect on your life and see if there have been people in your life who have bullied, victimised or slandered you. It may seem like you've had no break in your life from this kind of treatment. All these experiences stack up, one on top of each other, and morph into one overwhelming experience. Because they've happened so often, it becomes almost impossible to isolate each event.

It all started with my dad being overprotective and possessive —to a level that was smothering. I was not allowed to go out or stay over at friends' houses. As far as parties were concerned, they were limited. It was such a difficult time to overcome. Aside from the restricted freedom, I couldn't help but feel like I wasn't trusted. I was made to feel irresponsible, and that hurt me. In a way, I wasn't responsible to some extent, as I couldn't make independent decisions. If my dad didn't approve of what I wanted to do, then I couldn't do it. This was even more intense because of the level of emotional deprivation my dad had lacked in his own life.

The emotional pain I experienced from my dad affected me throughout my childhood, so let's fast forward to my forties, when I was planning to get married. My dad was such a hard man. He showed no interest during one of the most important decisions of my life. I expected him to have a sit-down chat with my fiancé—the usual steps of: "Let's sit down and talk about your intentions for my daughter" conversation—but this never happened.

I never felt or got his approval—the type all girls desire from their father at such an important stage in their lives. I did not experience that sort of joy or happiness. I mean, I was with someone I wanted to share my life with, but my dad couldn't see that. It was an unbelievable feeling.

He wasn't even interested in talking to me and was dismissive. I felt he was being very self-absorbed, and it hurt. I did find out later that he had his concerns, which was great, but he didn't share that with me. I needed to talk, but we only talked about it whenever I brought it up, and even then he shut the conversations down quickly.

FIRST CARD DROPPED AND EVERYTHING FOLLOWED

So the pain I felt from his lack of interest was so severe at a time when I should be glowing with overwhelming joy. It was even more intense, because there were also other things going on, which highlighted my mother's absence even more, as she had passed twenty years earlier. So, there was nobody else I could turn to but my dad for that validation. I had feared my dad all my life, and that has made me feel inferior. I felt a lot of shame and guilt, especially because of how hurtful his words could be. I can remember one major incident vividly during the planning of my wedding, my dad passed away in November 2010, whilst we were planning our wedding which was to happen the following year. So my wedding had to be put on hold, to plan for the funeral. As you can imagine, there was a lot of pain and negative emotions at this time. Despite how he had treated me, he was still my father. I moved back into the family home for six months before my wedding. The level of stress was off the scale and, as if that were not enough, I was made redundant one month before my wedding. You can imagine this was a lot to deal with at one time, Lord! It was like once the first card in the pack dropped, everything followed.

It was a very sad time. My father had never showed me the kind of love that you'd expect from a parent—I never felt good enough. The lack of positive affirmation had a major impact on my self-image. The fact that I was getting married was a miracle, as it proved a lot of the work I had gone through had brought a lot of internal healing in my life. The invisible wall that encased my heart had fallen and made room for someone to be able to reach my heart and love me for me. I only heard how my dad was proud of me from other people. He had informed others, but he never told me how proud he was of me to my face.

PATHWAYS TO HEALING:
Overcoming Childhood Trauma and Adult Pain of Sibling Estrangement

All I got from him was endless criticism. I think you get the picture. As I mentioned before, I was a highly sensitive child and was aware of other people's emotions. I've since realised that I was an empath. If you can identify with being one as well, you'll know we always want to help people and help out with whatever was making them so sad or upset. I have now realised this is a positive gift that I possess.

Being sensitive has helped me realise my uniqueness. I've come to realise it is my gift, and it is in no way a negative thing. So, when people mock you for who you are, never buckle or crumble under the weight of their ridicule. Don't let their jest or mockery shape you. Even if what you are doing is considered a bad thing, make sure you change on your terms, not theirs. Let me give you an example of another incident that happened when I was eight.

In most Caribbean homes, as I've mentioned (or you may already be aware), we had to complete our chores before any leisure activity could begin. On this particular day, a Saturday morning, I remember my dad was out in the backyard, doing some carpentry work. It was again another tense day, where I was being picked on for no apparent reason. So I went out to the backyard and asked my dad the following question: "Who has hurt you so much, that you have to hurt me so much?" At that time, I had had enough of the emotional abuse, although I didn't know that's what it was called at the time. There was no response from him. Parents consciously or unconsciously put their insecurities onto their children and don't make amends. This can distort how the child's self-image develops as they grow. My mum was a quiet person and, over some time, she became a Christian and grew into a new strength that I admired.

In one way or another, we all have negative feelings or hurts stemming from either, or both, of our parents. An emotional void is left as a consequence. Maybe your dad or mum treated you differently from your other siblings. Maybe you're the first child, the middle child but, wherever you fit, you're worthy of love. They didn't give you the same level of attention or support, and so you felt unloved. This can leave a severe negative imprint in your mind about how you see and feel about yourself. Your self-worth and acceptance are marred by feelings of unworthiness and being unlovable, or you're not good enough, or something is wrong with you. This is how you see yourself, which negatively impacts your life. Yes, some people will see you in a negative light, and that's their perspective, but the most important view you need to be concerned about is *God's* view of you, and *your* view of you.

Any other view is none of your business! Let's look at it in different ways. Perhaps your parents received the same treatment from their parents when they were growing up, so if they did, this would make a whole lot of sense. If their parents mistreated them, it explains why they don't know how to support or love you in the way you want. Never let how your parents treated you define your life. You can always emerge as a better person, despite the horrible treatment you received. Just decide that enough is enough, and that you want to take the path towards your healing.

CHAPTER SEVEN:

BLAME & SHAME

When I talk about emotional abuse, it is because I understand it. I know it like the back of my hand. (I hope that doesn't sound too cliché.) Unfortunately, I lived this life for so many years, and it is not the kind of life I would wish on anyone. Despite numerous years of emotional abuse, its effects still kept showing up in some of my relationships, because I found it hard to trust others, particularly men. As I grew older, it affected my self-esteem and self-worth. Whenever I questioned those who hurt me, I would sometimes blame myself and feel ashamed for asking the questions. I felt I was rejected. Was it because there was something wrong with me, even though I couldn't understand why that would be the case? This meant I was questioning my very existence, that there must be something wrong with me as a person, which was false.

The Bible mentions the word 'shame' over four hundred and thirty-one times. That's a lot of times, and lets me know that God wants us to overcome it, and that it's a big issue for the human race to deal with. So many people now are being shamed on social media to such extremes that there are no filters on what people can and can't say. What I have come to understand is that the people who treated me in such a bad way had no real basis for the way they were treating me. They didn't take responsibility for their shortcomings, and they blamed me for both their bad experiences and for what they were lacking in their own lives. They knew what they were doing, and their choices and actions caused a web of distrust, disconnecting them from the tragic consequences it created in my life. They didn't realise that how they were treating me affected my well-being... or maybe they did. I was increasingly becoming a negative person, and I lost my laughter and joy for life. Can you identify with that? But I thank God that He has already vindicated me from these accusations.

"There is therefore now no condemnation to those who are in Jesus Christ, who do not walk according to the flesh, but according to the Spirit. For the law of the Spirit of life in Jesus Christ has made me free from the law of sin and death." – Romans 8:1-2 (NKJV)

I hope that if you're experiencing blame and shame, you will be able to make sense of it and use the tools provided in this book to start rebuilding your life. In comparison, not understanding what is happening is worse than feeling the pains of rejection. That alone can drive you into an unstable situation.

Although it can hit you like a boulder, once you realise that you have been experiencing emotional abuse, you can begin to understand why this is happening. It's one of the hardest things to face, but there is a way for you to handle it without letting it break you. With the help of God, you can start taking steps to stop revisiting the experiences in your mind. All the difficult situations you've gone through with that individual or those groups of people can change your life, but you can live free. I know it's hard to stop the negative chatter and feelings from replaying in your mind but, with help, you can change, otherwise it can destroy you from the inside out.

May I suggest you ask God to take away the pain and the disappointment that you've experienced? Ask Him to heal your broken heart. It might not happen immediately, but He will restore your inner health, peace and joy. Listen to the words of encouragement from Isaiah 61:3 (NIV) – "*...and provide for those who grieve in Zion—to bestow on them a crown of beauty instead of ashes, the oil of joy instead of mourning, and a garment of praise instead of a spirit of despair.*"

God wants you to be whole and well, so you can enjoy your life again. He doesn't wish for anyone to go through difficult situations. But, He can use it for your good. He wants you to be complete again. He is always ready to help anyone who looks to Him for help. I want you to know you can rise from the crippling pain and move forward with your life. If He sent His Son to redeem humankind, do you think there's anything He will not do to make sure that you're happy and fulfilled? You just need to make the decision that it's your time to come out of whatever hole you are in. Nothing can change until you make a decision. Once you're clear about this and you seek the right help, you'll see unspeakable and unimaginable changes in your life. We can't be our own counsellors for too long, so get help from a trusted friend or professional, who can help you see things differently and put you on your journey to wholeness. There is no shame in asking for help.

Les Brown says, "Ask for help; not because you are weak, but because you want to remain strong." For those of you who may not know who Les Brown is, he is one of the world's most renowned motivational speakers, and I have had the privilege of meeting him twice in my life: once in the UK and the other time in the USA, which was awesome!

He has many quotes that empower you to renew your mind and live your best life, despite what you've gone through. I'm sure you have a lot of pent-up emotions; you may be angry, sad or feeling hopeless. But push through, and stay on this path of healing. Remember, you are still walking on your journey to healing and, at first, it will be difficult and too hard to face. Stay focused! Let's continue to move forward through another part of the maze, by doing the action steps that will look at your past experiences.

BLAME & SHAME

ACTION STEPS

1. Can you identify with whom, and where you've received most of the blame and shame?

   _____
   _____
   _____
   _____

2. How does this make you feel?

   _____
   _____
   _____
   _____

3. How would you like these feelings to be changed?

   _____
   _____
   _____
   _____

4. What steps will you take towards your healing?

   _____
   _____
   _____
   _____

PATHWAYS TO HEALING:
Overcoming Childhood Trauma and Adult Pain of Sibling Estrangement

CHAPTER EIGHT:
CASTING ASIDE IMAGINATIONS

*P*athways to Healing is my story of overcoming my past and triumphantly carving a brighter present and future. It's not fully complete yet, but my past does not hurt as much as it used to. I know I will reach a place where I'm completely free from the effects of the pain. May you be inspired to walk your pathway of healing so that you can write your own story?

Let me take some time to remind you of who you are. You are stronger than you can even begin to comprehend. You can accomplish more than you could ever dream. All the pain, tears, sorrows, rejection and confusion will work out for your good. How do I know that? In Romans 8:28 [NIV] – *"And we know that in all things God works for the good of those who love Him, who have been called according to His purpose."* We may not be able to understand how all these experiences will come together and work for our good; only God knows this.

All you should know is that it will work out for you in the end, and this is a wonderful hope. There are things we all have to do for healing to reach our hearts and soul. One of those things to consider is to allow God to come into your situation and let Him help you heal.

PATHWAYS TO HEALING:
Overcoming Childhood Trauma and Adult Pain of Sibling Estrangement

You may feel anger towards God for not stopping the action of others that caused the pain you've experienced before it happened. I understand that, and it's okay to feel like that. What we don't understand is how He can make a bad situation into a good one. Things happen to us; they just do.

But He can turn all your pain, rejection and disappointment into something good through the power of His love. Can you make room for Him so He can heal, remould and turn it around for your good?

There are many promises in the Book of Psalms that will encourage you to believe that nothing you've gone through will be in vain. So, for those moments when you're feeling discouraged, it's a book that can get your spirits up. These promises provide assurances, in case you still doubt that you have the power to overcome. Since God has given us these promises, you can claim them as your own. They have helped me to start believing new truths, which have brought new hope for my future.

Psalms 34:4-6[NIV] – *"I sought the LORD, and He answered me; He delivered me from all my fears. Those who look to Him are radiant; their faces are never covered with shame. This poor man called, and the LORD heard him; He saved him out of all his troubles."*

Psalms 34:18[NIV] – *"The LORD is close to the broken-hearted and saves those who are crushed in spirit."*

CASTING ASIDE IMAGINATIONS

I understand that rationalising how all the pain you've gone through will work out for your good might sound strange. However, you should know that this is a supernatural act. Our mere human minds are incapable of understanding how this will happen. You just need to know that no experience is in vain, and the end will be greater than the beginning. Things may even turn out better than you dreamed. Once you let the love of God take the place of your pain, thus changing your focus towards Him, you will be able to come out of those dark times. His love will shine light into the deepest parts of your pain, and things will begin to turn around for your good. One of the first things is to implement the following task into our lives, which is: *"We demolish arguments and every pretension that sets itself up against the knowledge of God, and we take captive every thought to make it obedient to Christ."* – 2 Corinthians 10:5 (NIV)

We play a part in our healing. The Scripture above talks about demolishing arguments. It refers to words and discussions that go on in our minds—also referred to as self-talk. Becoming aware of what we are thinking begins the journey towards changing our lives from the inside out. If you think you are nothing, then your self-esteem will be low. We can end up abusing ourselves, alongside other people who will also take advantage of us and emotionally use and abuse us. If you can start changing the way you both think and talk to yourself, your life will match your words.

PATHWAYS TO HEALING:
Overcoming Childhood Trauma and Adult Pain of Sibling Estrangement

Henry Ford said, *"Whether you think you can, or you think you can't, you're right."* Don't you just love that, if you say *"I am beautiful,"* *"I am enough,"* and *"I can do it,"* you'll see changes like never before.

So, there is a great level of self-power that you can give yourself. There is a place you can get to, and use the pain you've gone through as fuel to propel you forward into a life of joy and fulfilment. These definitions of control and pain will help you navigate through your maze. I mention them often, as they are key to what you've experienced. They will help you become more empowered rather than disempowered when dealing with the pain you've experienced. Additionally, they will help you take steps towards your journey of healing. So what do control and pain mean? Let's look at the explanations:

CONTROL – the power to influence or direct people's behaviour or the course of events.

PAIN – an experience characterised by a highly distressing sensation in a particular part of the body. It can also be mental pain, emotional suffering or torment.

At this moment, I just want to remind you that you are more than a conqueror. On our own, we're weak, and only God can give us what we can't give ourselves. I would like you to consider allowing the new resources to help you today, to start turning your pain around. You have come this far, so you might as well emerge a changed and better person. Take time to look back and see how far you have come. You are powerful. What came to break you in the first place will be what causes you to look back and see how far you have come. It will be used as fuel to make your life better.

PATHWAYS TO HEALING:
Overcoming Childhood Trauma and Adult Pain of Sibling Estrangement

CHAPTER NINE:

WHOLE IN EVERY PART

Dreams are beautiful. I love the way they provide answers we cannot explore while awake. I dream occasionally, and I always find assurance and specific answers I need at the time. As a consequence of this, I expect to have them frequently in my life. Dreams are amazing and powerful.

"For God does speak—now one way, now another—though no one perceives it. In a dream, in a vision of the night, when deep sleep falls on people as they slumber in their beds, He may speak in their ears and terrify them with warnings, to turn them from wrongdoing and keep them from pride, to preserve them from the pit, their lives from perishing by the sword." – Job 33:14-18 (NIV)

On a day-to-day basis, our subconscious mind directs our individual lives as well as stores all our past experiences. Therefore, at night when we sleep, it causes us to dream and brings us solutions to problems we might face when we are awake. This element of our subconscious is a testament to how amazing our mind is. It is little wonder that even science cannot comprehend its power. Our mind is an incomprehensible entity that provides answers to the everyday challenges we face. Aside from this, it also provides us with strategies and the blueprint that empowers us to change our lives and make an impact on the lives of the people who live around us. Our subconscious mind presents solutions to us as coded information that matches the challenges we face. It is our source connected to a higher power, and through it, we are provided with solutions from the spiritual realm. God also uses our dreams to give us direction, so we don't take the wrong path or make the wrong decisions.

We can be equally influenced by negative spirits, where we don't have positive or helpful dreams. I say all this because I have experienced them, and I'm sure you have too. I have received some amazing and on-point answers, solutions and revelations through some of the dreams I've had over the years.

One thing I can tell you is this: we all have different gifts, like prophecy, words of knowledge, and through them they can help us to get answers to our problems and life challenges. Dreams are one of these gifts. If you have this ability, what has helped me is to keep a journal, as well as writing down my dreams, and seek God's interpretation of them. In the next section, I would like to share with you a dream I had in July 2015, which I've entitled 'Suspended Tree with Teardrops'.

This dream tells of an amazing experience, which has had a significant impact on my life to this day. In the dream, I saw a tree suspended in mid-air, with very large teardrops hanging from its branches. These teardrops looked like lots of amniotic sacs (the fluid-filled sac that protects a foetus in the womb), commonly called the bag of waters. There were quite a number of them hanging from the ends of the branches. I understood that each tear must represent a dream, desire or expectation. I also understood that the amniotic sacs were waiting to be delivered; all the tears were gathered and waiting to be released. Then, from nowhere, I heard "PUSH." It says in Psalms 56:8 (NKJV): "You number my wanderings. Put my tears into Your bottle. Are they not in Your book?"

If you look at this dream, on the face of it, it carries little meaning. But, as I looked into it, it carried a lot of powerful hope and reassurance for me. What the dream was telling me was this: God has caught all my tears, and not one has been wasted. Isn't that amazing? If God is good, then all that He has for me is also good. Therefore, I want all that is good in my book to now be manifested in my life! What about you? We go through so many unpleasant things in life that we sometimes have to stop and evaluate our responses. If you are experiencing deep pain that consumes you, it will eventually cause you to stop dreaming. It'll prevent you from living a full life, and it'll stop you from achieving your heart's desires.

PATHWAYS TO HEALING:
Overcoming Childhood Trauma and Adult Pain of Sibling Estrangement

You'll just become a sack of hurtful experiences, hurting not only yourself but those around you. In life, we all have to make certain choices. Some choices are easier to make than others, but that's a part of life. Pain numbs our thinking. It recalibrates our mind, and warps it so much that we think there are no good choices left. It takes us into a swirling vortex of previous bad experiences, and all we do is make one bad decision after another. This is why you need to use your power as fuel to regain control over your life.

If you don't seek healing and continue to let the pain control you, the consequences will be an unlived life. If you think there are no good choices left, you'll begin to live in the lie your pain has created.

So, if you want to get your life back on track—if you want to snatch your power back from the claws of pain—you can decide to find healing. This begins with forgiving those who hurt you. You can decide to continue to feel bad about what they did, or you can forgive them. We can find that for our healing to take place, forgiveness plays a part in it. It does not mean that others shouldn't be held accountable for what they have done to us, but the process is to help us change our focus and move forward through the maze of our hurt. Now you can choose to do the same to the people who have offended you. Forgiveness can be a long process but, once we begin our journey towards it, things get easier.

Forgiveness is needed and cannot be negotiated if you truly want to be free. When you forgive, it's for your freedom, and you can decide to let go of the pain. Forgiveness does not mean you agree to what happened or have let the person off; it's about you releasing yourself from the bondage the pain has kept you in. Then, and only then, are you able to begin to focus on more productive things for your life and build your happiness. Also, we have to choose to forgive ourselves by receiving God's forgiveness that is available to us at any hour of the day. We just have to learn to ask for it. The journey we take to have a more fulfilling life always comes with lots of difficulties.

A crucial step in your healing process is to gauge how you're feeling about yourself, and to decide where you are right now. It might be challenging to identify who you are, especially when you've gone through so much. As you delve further into this book, you will find how crucial the gift of dreams was to the story of Joseph. This is something we will explore at length throughout the pages of this book. God gave Joseph a dream, and everything from that moment in his life completely changed. So, I'm going to give you some action steps that will help you identify how you see yourself. It will help you to see where you currently are on the map of your journey. I think it will help to understand that there is power in a name, so what does Joseph's name mean? This will bring context to the story, so let's see what it means in the next chapter —and think about the meaning of your name as well.

ACTION STEPS

Focus on You

Just for a moment, let's separate you from your family, friends, and associates:

1. Whom do you think you are (your character, likes, dislikes or beliefs)?

   _____
   _____
   _____
   _____

2. What type of person do you want to be?

   _____
   _____
   _____
   _____

3. How has your character changed over the years?

   _____
   _____
   _____
   _____

4. When you think about yourself, is the first thought negative? If so, why?

   _____
   _____

5. What changes do you want to see in your life?

PATHWAYS TO HEALING:
Overcoming Childhood Trauma and Adult Pain of Sibling Estrangement

CHAPTER TEN:
POWER IN A NAME

I have an interest in knowing what people's names mean. In the Bible, the name given to a person was very important; it was like a proclamation to define the destiny which that person would live out. A name can define and shape a person's life purpose.

As if, by instinct, most parents with newborn babies take their time to decide on the name of the child —whether it will be a continuation of the family name, like Christopher III, or a new name. You can think of this as an important rite of passage for all parents. So I would like to share with you the meanings of my names, as follows:

Carmen - means garden, **Patricia** means noble and **Carrol** means warrior. Let's break down what each one means:

Garden is a piece of land next to or around your house, where you can grow flowers, fruit and vegetables.

Noble is having or showing fine personal qualities that people admire, such as courage, honesty and care for others, or belonging to a family of high social rank.

Warrior is a brave or experienced soldier or fighter.

So, I am a noble garden and I am a warrior. Yes! I agree and love the explanations of my names. I believe my life (my garden) will be fruitful, because my tears have watered my garden for so many years. I think I'm courageous, and honest, and I am a warrior for peace and truth!

What does your name mean? It can be important that you find out, as it can help to identify with who you are. So some people in the Bible had a name change, because God no longer wanted them to be identified with the name they were given at birth, or to be seen as a sum of what they've gone through, or how others saw them. (Although I'm not suggesting in any way that you have to change your name, OK? Just so we're clear!)

In the case of Joseph, his name means 'increase or addition'. Knowing this, I then asked myself: why was he experiencing so much famine in his life? I think it's important to mention here that Joseph did eventually get married whilst he was in exile. And he had two sons. He called them Manasseh and Ephraim. The meaning of their names is evidence of how much healing he had gone through. The explanation of their names is as follows:

Manasseh meant 'causing to forget', and Ephraim meant 'fruitful'.

Despite all he went through, he arrived at a place in his life where he was willing to let it all go - to allow God to help him forget all the troubles he had gone through in his father's house. He was able to live and become fruitful in the place that caused so much pain. I want to forget all I went through, so that I too can be fruitful.

We pick up the story in Genesis 37:1-4[NLT]: *'So Jacob settled again in the land of Canaan, where his father had lived as a foreigner.*

'This is the account of Jacob and his family. When Joseph was seventeen years old, he often tended his father's flocks. He worked for his half-brothers, the sons of his father's wives Bilhah and Zilpah. But Joseph reported to his father some of the bad things his brothers were doing.

'Jacob loved Joseph more than any of his other children, because Joseph had been born to him in his old age. So one day, Jacob had a special gift made for Joseph—a beautiful robe. But his brothers hated Joseph, because their father loved him more than the rest of them. They couldn't say a kind word to him.'

I want to focus on the word 'hate' here for a while. Of all the words that could have been used, the writer chose 'hate', so let's break it down…

The following words are synonyms for HATE: feel intense dislike for, loathe, detest, dislike greatly, abhor, abominate, despise, feel aversion towards, feel revulsion towards, feel hostile towards, be repelled by, be revolted by, regard with disgust, not be able to bear/stand, be unable to stomach, and find intolerable (Oxford Dictionaries Online).

I don't think I need to talk much on the issue of hate, because it's something everyone has experienced in one shape or another. Even Jesus was hated and despised. I share in **Chapter Thirteen** some of the comparisons between the life of Joseph and Jesus. So, what did Joseph do to warrant such a level of hatred from his brothers? Psalm 69:4(NIV) says: "*Those who hate me without reason outnumber the hairs of my head; many are my enemies without cause, those who seek to destroy me. I am forced to restore what I did not steal.*"

Looking at the story of Joseph, it's obvious he was an honest and self-righteous person. He couldn't stand by and watch as bad things happened. His personality wouldn't allow it. I'm sure we can all relate to this in one way or another. Perhaps you've been in many situations where you couldn't sit back, so you took it upon yourself to do something to prevent or stop something bad taking place. For example, you spoke out against an unusual situation that is happening in your family, which warranted some of your family members to hate you. This is very similar to what happened to Joseph.

When his brothers did something bad, Joseph could neither stand it nor cover it up. So, he told their father about it. You can say he used his favour against his brothers because he knew that his dad would protect him. You can say he took advantage of being his father's favourite, because Jacob did not hide his love for Joseph. You can make these theories and they might be true. However, the facts we can verify are that Joseph was a righteous man, and he was hated by his brothers for this. This was the same reason his father loved him so much more than he loved his other eleven sons and daughters.

I can say with much certainty that showing favouritism for one child over the other as a parent is not the right thing to do. This is because it can potentially affect the development of the child. I am sure a lot of you can identify with either being the favourite child or not the favourite child.

Whichever one you can identify with, you may agree or disagree that it has a mixed impact and consequences on your life and the family. The dynamics can also be different across some families who just ignore it altogether.

In some families, they express their feelings about favouritism. In others, they hold resentment in their hearts, and never express their discontent and jealousy. Then, over time, the floodgates of hatred and anger burst open. I don't know about you, but it is sad to know some of your family members hold hateful feelings towards you, and they act as though they don't. One can only tolerate this for so long before a decision is necessary to move on with your life.

PATHWAYS TO HEALING:
Overcoming Childhood Trauma and Adult Pain of Sibling Estrangement

CHAPTER ELEVEN:
I AM

So now you know the meaning of your name. Did it surprise you, or did you already know what it meant? What I want you to do now is a simple and powerful task: I would like you to make some affirmations (or decrees that some may prefer to call them). I'll ask you to do some action steps; a quiet space is the best place for this. However, if you're in a public space where you can't get any privacy, you can do these action steps in your mind.

You can add to the ones I've listed. These are just to aid you to start working on changing your mind. Let's look at some of these affirmations or decrees. You will be directing these affirmations at your pain, so that you can begin your healing process. Here it goes:

- I am able to live my life better and stronger.
- I am strong enough to take back control of my life.
- I am able to decide to live my life in peace and with direction.
- I am choosing to be free from this pain.
- I will know the truth, and this truth will set me free.

PATHWAYS TO HEALING:
Overcoming Childhood Trauma and Adult Pain of Sibling Estrangement

Repeat these statements as often as you can; you can write them on a card, or you can just download them from my website. I have created some for both men and women. This will help your mind to gradually move away from the effects of a negative way of thinking, and will help your mind focus on healing.

'I am' statements are very powerful - it's a sure and sound statement. They create a psychological effect of possibility in your mind. And when you want to heal, you cannot remind yourself enough that you can do it. In Job 22:28 [NIV], it says: *'What you decide on will be done, and light will shine on your ways.'*

To understand how important and powerful 'I am' statements are, Jesus used them several times in His life. In a sermon, Billy Graham, who was a prominent Christian evangelist in the 1940s, outlines seven times where Jesus used an 'I am' statement in the Gospel of John. The sermon can be found on decisionmagazine.com.

- He said, *"I AM the **bread of life**. Whoever comes to me will never go hungry..."* in John 6:35[NIV]. He was letting us know that He was, and is, the substance that fills the hungry soul; that He was the only one who could satisfy the human need for God.

- Jesus said, *"I AM the **light of the world**,"* John 8:12[NIV]. Living in a dark world because of sin, He tells us that He is the light that leads us back to God.

- He said, *"I AM **the door**,"* John 10:9 (NKJV). He is the only entry into heaven - the only entry point to God.

- He said, *"I AM the **good shepherd**. The good shepherd lays down his life for the sheep,"* John 10:11 (NIV). He is good and looks after those who are His.

- Jesus said in John 11:25 (NIV), *"I AM the **resurrection and the life**".* He is eternal life, and there is life in no other person or thing.

- He said, *"I AM **the way**, the **truth**, and the **life**. No one comes to the Father except through me,"* John 14:6 (NIV). The only way that all humankind can experience God is through Jesus. He is the truth that sets us free, and the giver and sustainer of all living things.

- He said, in John 15:1 (NIV) that He is our source.

So, if Jesus is all these 'I AMs', what else can He be? Whatever He wants to be, this list is not exhausted. Also, He can be all we need Him to be—at any time or in any circumstances we may be facing. If we need to feel the love of a father, mother, brother or sister, if we need a healer, a comforter, He can be that for us. God's greatest desire is to be in a relationship with us, and He will use any incident to speak to us. He will use the Holy Spirit—don't be alarmed, it's not a 'spooky' spirit—the gentle and the third Person of the Godhead, who represents and expresses the love and comfort of God to us. He uses other people to encourage us – to receive His Son,

Jesus Christ, into our lives as He offers you a life in all its fullness. His arms are always open, to receive you just as you are, wherever you are, whatever you've gone through, to receive the gift of His forgiveness for sins, and to give you life in all its fullness. All you need to do is ask Him into your life and situation. The question now is this: will you make this life-changing commitment?

Committing yourself to God enables you to set your sights and thoughts on Him and the perspective He has of your life, which includes new hope. If you are not interested in making a decision, that is your choice. (Thanks for reading to this point.) The truth is that focusing on your pain and hurt only magnifies it – it makes it bigger than it should be. If you focus on God, instead of magnifying your problem, you magnify Him. As you do this, your problems start to diminish immensely. I know that changing your focus is important to achieve complete healing.

In **Chapter Twenty**, I detail how my body reacted while going through several illnesses due to the stress I was under. I do suggest throughout this book how you can manage your pain. Some of these suggestions will help you consider some simple questions when dealing with traumatic events in one's life. This process can sometimes be equally as painful, because it can feel like you are reliving it. But, like everything else in life, unless you're willing to stop and face your fears, you won't overcome them. So, what are you putting up with? What is it you tolerate that you can't complain about? Now is the time for you to free yourself and live your life without constraints. What do you owe yourself? Is it the time you have lost worrying over what happened? Or is it the forgiveness over the resentment and guilt you've carried in your mind? Have you lost your peace, where every waking moment replays the pain you've experienced? Have you ever wanted lasting and intimate relationships and love, but didn't receive them due to the invisible wall that encased your heart? Or is it the love you want to give, but it doesn't work out because you've been rejected?

It is time to take back control of your time, peace and love, and to be grateful for surviving what you have gone through. This is your opportunity to be free to make your own choices without the influence of your tragic past or current experience.

PATHWAYS TO HEALING:
Overcoming Childhood Trauma and Adult Pain of Sibling Estrangement

CHAPTER TWELVE:
CHARACTER BUILDING EQUALS PAIN

When we take Joseph's life at face value, it seems as though he was losing out on many things rather than gaining. But his major increase, which was not evident at the time but would later be a positive addition to his life, was that his character was being developed and prepared for a future purpose.

In my life, it felt that I lost a lot and didn't know it would be possible to have lost so much. As human beings, we tend to calculate prosperity in monetary terms. While things such as getting a nice house and a fancy car are good, they are not enough to measure prosperity. We should think of success and prosperity in terms of something more valuable than money.

When we think of Joseph's story, I sometimes see myself; it's the inspiration that gives me hope. So is there anyone that you identify with? Is there someone's story that gives you the hope you need to keep going? Just like he had a greater purpose to fulfil, we do too, but for this to happen, we all have to be prepared, and some of this does include pain and difficulties. Our discernment has to be heightened and our wisdom has to be developed. We have to foster our area of gifting - be it dream interpretation, prophecy or words of knowledge - which is crucial to achieving our purpose and providing us with strategies to solve problems.

So, everything we went through - the difficulties and challenges we encountered - can shape and prepare us for our purpose. We had to go through the process of refinement, just like gold. When you look at it from this perspective, you'll realise that there will be a lot of increase in the end. So if you feel like you're currently going through a lot of pain, and you don't seem to be making headway, just make some slight manageable changes in your thinking and life. Just like the story of Joseph, his pain started to change and was not in vain, and it'll work for you in the end too.

Another aspect I want to focus on in Joseph's story is his father's love. His father, Jacob, loved Joseph, and didn't hide his favouritism. This was made more obvious when Jacob gave Joseph a unique gift in the form of a seamless, multi-coloured coat. As mentioned, he was the eleventh son of twelve brothers and sisters. Joseph had two dreams, which would unfold over many years. These dreams would lead him to fulfil his purpose and destiny. Before he was sold into slavery, it was commonplace to share your dreams with others, to get an interpretation. So, he shared his two dreams with his family.

CHARACTER BUILDING EQUALS PAIN

Genesis 37:5-11(NIV) *– "Joseph had a dream and, when he told it to his brothers, they hated him all the more. *[6]* He said to them, 'Listen to this dream I had: *[7]* We were binding sheaves of grain out in the field when suddenly my sheaf rose and stood upright, while your sheaves gathered around mine and bowed down to it.' *[8]* His brothers said to him, 'Do you intend to reign over us? Will you actually rule us?' And they hated him all the more because of his dream and what he had said. *[9]* Then he had another dream, and he told it to his brothers. 'Listen,' he said, 'I had another dream, and this time the sun and moon and eleven stars were bowing down to me.' *[10]* When he told his father as well as his brothers, his father rebuked him and said, 'What is this dream you had? Will your mother and I and your brothers actually come and bow down to the ground before you?' *[11]* His brothers were jealous of him, but his father kept the matter in mind."*

Joseph had experienced sibling rejection and consequently was estranged from his family for years. He experienced both pain and trauma because his brothers had been jealous of him from an early age, and hated him even before he spoke of his dreams. But after they knew about his dreams, the hatred grew even more. To them, it became imperative to take him out of the equation as quickly as possible to prevent his dreams from coming to pass. But they didn't know they were simply pushing him towards his destiny. For Joseph, it marked the beginning of his seventeen years of adult pain, trauma, imprisonment, rejection, accusation, isolation and famine. Eventually, this led to his path to healing and to promotion, release, increase and addition after his many years of suffering.

Let me ask you, how long have you been waiting to see an increase in your life? For some of you, it seems like forever. To others, you've even given up. Some have even come to accept that they are not meant for great things. But if Joseph could become a great person after going through so much suffering, you can too. So don't give up hope. Never give up hope.

What challenges are you facing right now? What challenges have you faced in the past? I want you to consider the following points and issues Joseph had to contend with, yet he came out soaring:

- Joseph never felt like he fitted in with his family.

- Joseph experienced his father's unconditional love. He knew his dad favoured him.

- Joseph was the eleventh son of more than twelve siblings.

- Joseph's siblings didn't love him unconditionally.

- Joseph had a dream, and it showed him what was going to happen in the future.

This is what I encountered in my own life;

- I never felt like I fitted in with my family.

CHARACTER BUILDING EQUALS PAIN

- I never experienced the unconditional love of my father.

- I was the eighth child of eight siblings.

- Some of my siblings loved me conditionally.

- I've had dreams that showed me what was happening in my life.

Have you ever experienced any of these situations?

Feeling like you never fitted in with your family?

Receiving conditional or unconditional love from your father or mother?

Never feeling the unconditional love from some of your siblings?

Knowing God has a plan, but you were not sure what it was?

Somehow, you knew you were different—not different in just natural features, which makes us all unique, but you just knew there was something about you that was special. Yet, everything around you is telling you a very different story.... Joseph's future would involve him overseeing a food bank distribution centre during a famine like Egypt had never experienced before. All his life's experiences were preparing him for a meeting with Pharaoh, the ruler of Egypt. So during all the time Joseph had experienced rejection, pain, disappointment, and confusion, he did not know that in one moment in time, in twenty-four hours, his gift would bring him before the ruler of Egypt, and that he would have the answer to a problem no one else could answer. This knowledge would elevate him to a place of prominence like nothing had before. When we look at the story of Joseph, it shows redemption, forgiveness, provision, increase and freedom. He did not know that the plan for his life was unfolding. He was not aware of what it was, but knew he just did not fit in. He knew he was different. He was anointed or had favour in his life, and this required that he needed the character to fulfil his purpose; unfortunately, this included going through some painful moments.

Yet everything around him was telling him something different. So, what made him so special? The dreams Joseph had and shared with his father and his siblings were the first steps towards his destiny unfolding. He had a destiny, and so do you.

DESTINY is described as 'the events that will happen to a particular person at some appointed time in the future. The hidden power believed to control future events; fate' (Oxford Dictionaries Online).

CHAPTER THIRTEEN:
JOSEPH & JESUS COMPARISONS

Mining for gold takes time and the associated processes are very tedious. First, it has to be extracted from the ground after years of prospecting. Then, it will be refined with fire, and the temperature can be roughly between 1000 and 1200 degrees Celsius. So when the gold reaches this extreme temperature, it melts and is palatable before it can be beaten into any desired design. Have you felt like you've gone through the fire of life and you've been beaten? This is just a summarised process that goes into mining pure and refined gold. Amazingly, this harsh but necessary process produces something beautiful! When we hear about or see gold, we rarely bother to consider the process it has passed through before it became something even more beautiful. Why am I saying this, you ask? It's because I want you to know that you are more precious than gold.

The challenges you go through are like the fire that refines you. The refining process will burn out the pain, hurt, negativity and any resistance within you. All of this is necessary for you to become your full self and achieve your destiny in life.

The journey we have to take to arrive at our destination can be one of the hardest things we could ever imagine. Achieving our dreams brings great lessons through the hardest pain. I hope that you will find your path to your place of breakthrough and freedom, wherever you are in your season.

Pathways to Healing is here to help you if you have experienced the immense pain of rejection that comes from those closest to you. Joseph's story prophetically represents the story of Jesus Christ in several ways— their stories represent suffering, authority, salvation and redemption, and we can learn a lot from their journey. I would like to just share with you some of the key comparisons between Joseph and Jesus, found on JewsforJesus.org.

I will list a few of the similarities between them:

1. They both knew the love of their Father:

"Now Israel loved Joseph more than any of his other sons…" Genesis 37:3 (NIV)

Isaac was also known as Israel. Remember, we talked about some people's names were changed in the Bible in Chapter Ten - Power in a Name.

"This is my Son, whom I love; with him, I am well pleased." Matthew 3:17 (NIV)

2. They were both given a coat that represented righteousness and authority:

"…they stripped him of his robe…" Genesis 37:23(NIV)

"They stripped him and put a scarlet robe on him…" Matthew 27:28(NIV)

3. They were both betrayed by their brothers:

"When his brothers saw that their father loved him more than any of them, they hated him…" Genesis 37:4(NIV)

"They hated me without reason." John 15:25(NIV)

4. They were both put into a pit:

"Then they took him, and cast him into a pit." Genesis 37:24(NKJV)

"…as Jonah was three days and three nights in the belly of the great fish, so will the Son of Man be three days and three nights in the heart of the earth." Matthew 12:40(ESV)

5. Their lives were sacrificed for others:

"…they plotted to kill him." Genesis 37:18(NIV)

"But they kept shouting, 'Crucify him! Crucify him!'…" Luke 23:21(NIV)

6. Their personalities were shaped through their suffering:

"Joseph's master took him and put him in prison, the place where the king's prisoners were confined." Genesis 39:20 (NIV)

"...there they crucified him, and the criminals, one on his right and one on his left." Luke 23:33 (ESV)

7. They led people out of suffering and certain death:

"And Pharaoh said to Joseph, 'See, I have set you over all the land of Egypt.'" Genesis 41:41 (ESV)

"...God exalted him to the highest place and gave him the name that is above every name..." Philippians 2:9 (NIV)

8. They redeemed and saved many through their suffering:

"You intended to harm me, but God intended it all for good. He brought me to this position so I could save the lives of many people." Genesis 50:20 (NLT)

"...who gave himself for us to redeem us from all wickedness and to purify for himself a people that are his very own, eager to do what is good." Titus 2:14 (NIV)

9. **Revelation and Reconciliation**: their lives had many similarities, which meant that their lives were pre-ordained. Additionally, what they went through resulted in them bringing reconciliation into other people's lives.

"Joseph said to his brothers, 'I am Joseph!'" Genesis 45:3 (NIV)

"The one who rescues will come from Jerusalem, and he will turn Israel away from ungodliness." Romans 11:26(NLT)

10. Their authority was maintained even in their suffering:

"This is what your son Joseph says: God has made me lord of all Egypt." Genesis 45:9

"Then Jesus came to them and said, "All authority in heaven and on earth has been given to Me." Matthew 28:18

The depth of rejection that Joseph experienced went deep. There is no form of rejection besides that of a parent rejecting you, greater than when your brothers or siblings intentionally sell you into slavery. Joseph, however, made the best of his situation. We get a glimpse of how he was feeling about where he was as we read the story. He was upset; of course he was.

Yet, during his pain, he was able to help others. Although he held a grudge against his brothers for a long time, let's be honest, he had to work through it. He lived through his pain and, because of that, he saved many people. You can read more about Joseph's story yourself in Genesis Chapters 37 and 39 to 45.

As I've said before, the story of Joseph fascinates me immensely. It helped me a lot to know that someone went through a similar experience to my own. At those times, when you're surviving, you just can't believe what you've gone through because your pain magnifies and consumes your life, and you can't see a way out of the maze! So his story started when he was seventeen years old, with some of the most uncommon experiences.

So, before we go further into this amazing story, I just want to ask you how you are feeling? I hope you're seeing now that there is hope in the midst of your situation, and that your sadness and disappointment can change. There is hope to love again, to believe again and to live again. So let's look a bit closer at the story of Joseph and the unfolding of his dream.

CHAPTER FOURTEEN:
JOSEPH SOLD BY HIS BROTHERS

We pick up the story in Genesis 37:12-36[(NIV)] – [12]*Now his brothers had gone to graze their father's flocks near Shechem,* [13] *and Israel said to Joseph, 'As you know, your brothers are grazing the flocks near Shechem. Come, I am going to send you to them.' 'Very well,' he replied.*

[14] *So he said to him, 'Go and see if all is well with your brothers and with the flocks, and bring word back to me.' Then he sent him off from the Valley of Hebron. When Joseph arrived at Shechem,* [15] *a man found him wandering around in the fields and asked him, 'What are you looking for?'* [16] *He replied, 'I'm looking for my brothers. Can you tell me where they are grazing their flocks?'* [17] *'They have moved on from here,' the man answered. 'I heard them say, "Let's go to Dothan." So, Joseph went after his brothers and found them near Dothan.* [18] *But they saw him in the distance, and before he reached them, they plotted to kill him.* [19] *'Here comes that dreamer!' they said to each other.*

[20] *'Come now, let's kill him and throw him into one of these cisterns and say that a ferocious animal devoured him. Then we'll see what comes of his dreams.'* [21] *When Reuben heard this, he tried to rescue him from their hands. 'Let's not take his life,' he said.* [22] *'Don't shed any blood. Throw him into this cistern here in the wilderness, but don't lay a hand*

on him.' Reuben said this to rescue him from them and take him back to his father.

²³ So when Joseph came to his brothers, they stripped him of his rob - the ornate robe he was wearing - ²⁴ and they took him and threw him into the cistern. The cistern was empty; there was no water in it. ²⁵ As they sat down to eat their meal, they looked up and saw a caravan of Ishmaelites coming from Gilead. Their camels were loaded with spices, balm, and myrrh, and they were on their way to take them down to Egypt.

²⁶ Judah said to his brothers, 'What will we gain if we kill our brother and cover up his blood? ²⁷ Come, let's sell him to the Ishmaelites and not lay our hands on him; after all, he is our brother, our own flesh and blood.' His brothers agreed.

²⁸ So when the Midianite merchants came by, his brothers pulled Joseph up out of the cistern and sold him for twenty shekels of silver to the Ishmaelites, who took him to Egypt. ²⁹ When Reuben returned to the cistern and saw that Joseph was not there, he tore his clothes. ³⁰ He went back to his brothers and said, 'The boy isn't there! Where can I turn now?'

³¹ Then they got Joseph's robe slaughtered a goat and dipped the robe in the blood. ³² They took the ornate robe back to their father and said, 'We found this. Examine it to see whether it is your son's robe.'

JOSEPH SOLD BY HIS BROTHERS

³³ He recognized it and said, 'It is my son's robe! Some ferocious animal has devoured him. Joseph has surely been torn to pieces.'

³⁴ Then Jacob tore his clothes put on sackcloth and mourned for his son many days. ³⁵ All his sons and daughters came to comfort him, but he refused to be comforted. 'No,' he said, 'I will continue to mourn until I join my son in the grave.' So, his father wept for him.

³⁶ Meanwhile, the Midianites sold Joseph in Egypt to Potiphar, one of Pharaoh's officials, the captain of the guard."

I think all the brothers were responsible for what happened to Joseph; they had already decided on several ways how they could hurt or kill Joseph. It was not a spur of the moment decision when they saw him coming towards them. The hate they had in their hearts consumed and overtook their minds for years, which led them to have a level of jealousy and resentment that would eventually need an outlet. They were just waiting for the right opportunity to present itself, so they could execute their devious plan. It was encouraging to see that some of his brothers started to stand up for him, and wanted to save him from his tragic fate, so he could be returned to the safety and protection of their father, but they were too late.

Remember I talked about Cain and Abel, and Jacob and Esau and that their feelings of rejection made them think and do unpalatable things towards their brothers. Again, we see nothing new here; Joseph's brothers also made the same decision to cause harm and they lied to themselves, they lied to God, and they lied to their father about what had happened. And they did not say sorry for what they did.

To understand the story of Joseph, you need to understand it as one big event. Only then can you make sense of the many different paths his life's journey took. I now know that it hurts so much more when you look at what you've gone through as just one small piece of the story.

Before Joseph came to the fulfilment of his destiny, many little things had to happen. As you'll have noticed, it didn't all happen in one day, but at specific times.

This is an encouragement for those of you who feel your life makes no sense. When you look at your life at a certain point in time, you perhaps will be unable to find meaning in it. But when you look at the culmination of previous events and what you've gone through to get to where you are now, you might be able to glean some more meaning to your life.

Joseph's brothers resented him even more after he shared the contents of his dreams. Hilariously, they were the ones who interpreted them, when they said that one day they would bow before him. Joseph's father kept the dream in his heart.

No one at the time knew the part each of them would play to make Joseph's dream come true. He experienced sibling rejection from a very young age. As bad as it was, neither he

JOSEPH SOLD BY HIS BROTHERS

nor his brothers and sisters knew how this was pushing him towards achieving his destiny. The sibling hurt that Joseph experienced gave him the platform needed to allow him to reign in a very powerful position in the future. At that time, this amazing outcome touched the whole of Egypt and saved many lives and his family for generations to come.

Bad things may be happening to you right now. You may be going through tough times in your life, and things may not be going right for you. It may have caused you so much pain and despair that you are already thinking of giving up. I'm asking you to persevere, as you look at the story of Joseph; glean some encouragement and motivation from it. Nothing happens without a purpose. Everything that is happening to you right now is by design. Don't you just dislike that cliché?

I do, but now I know that, in the end, it will all work out for your good. I know you're hurting, I know you're crying, I know you don't care anymore, but please don't give up! While Joseph was now in Egypt and seemingly prospering in a strange place, he began a 'food bank outreach programme' that would save people from years of famine. As this famine was ravaging Egypt, Joseph's high position didn't prevent him from feeling the effects of the famine. However, Joseph was contending with a different kind of famine. The disconnection from his immediate family affected every facet of his life. It prevented him from having and building a relationship with his brothers and sisters, and especially his father. He could no longer engage in conversations with them. Joseph was experiencing a relationship famine because he was alone in a strange land. There was no one to help him grow through adolescence and into maturity and manhood.

He had no one to guide him through this period. On top of this, he also experienced famine without home comforts and a sense of belonging. His position of influence didn't prevent him from feeling lonely. Despite his high position, he didn't feel like he belonged. His brother's famine at the time was a lack of food, which was nothing in comparison to what he was experiencing. What kind of famine have you experienced in your life? It might be quite a challenge to identify your places of famine, but I hope the following action steps will be of benefit, and direct you through the maze of your experiences.

JOSEPH SOLD BY HIS BROTHERS

ACTION STEPS

Identify Your Famine

1. In what areas of your life have you been experiencing famine? For example: -(relationships, opportunities, finances)

   _____
   _____
   _____
   _____

2. Whom do you need to forgive? *Forgiveness is not letting the other person(s) off for what they have done to you, it's an act of your will and it sets you free from reliving the pain.

   _____
   _____
   _____
   _____

3. What do you want God to restore in your life? (be realistic)

   _____
   _____
   _____
   _____

PATHWAYS TO HEALING:
Overcoming Childhood Trauma and Adult Pain of Sibling Estrangement

CHAPTER FIFTEEN:
SEEING THROUGH THE EYES OF PURPOSE

Before Joseph even had a dream, he was an innocent seventeen-year-old who was confident in who he was. So it all changed when he shared his dream with his family. He spoke it into being, and purpose was set into motion. He felt excluded from his family and did not fit in, which would have made him feel insignificant. Joseph was the person God wanted to use to complete a worldwide purpose.

His father, Jacob, showed his son regular expressions of love, and he had an awareness that his son had something special. This was expressed by giving him a special coat. There were three coats or cloaks that were given to Joseph. They all attracted some negative responses, but they all played a part in pushing him to his purpose.

PATHWAYS TO HEALING:
Overcoming Childhood Trauma and Adult Pain of Sibling Estrangement

THREE COATS AND CLOAKS:

What were the three coats and cloaks Joseph received that were important to each stage of his journey?

- The coat from his father – attracted jealousy.

- The cloak of authority he got from Potiphar – attracted sexual advances.

- The cloak that Pharaoh gave him – attracted him to be in charge of the national food bank.

All of these played a part in Joseph fulfilling his purpose; they showed he had a favour in his life that kept being challenged. So, not only did he receive three different types of coats or cloaks, but he was also thrown into two different prisons that left him alone and isolated. He had times in isolation away from his family and familiar surroundings. He had to deal with loneliness.

The first type of prison was the pit his brothers threw him into, which he was in for a few hours. Then his brothers sold him to the Ishmaelites. Then the Ishmaelites sold him to Potiphar, Captain of the Guards and, over time, Potiphar's wife showed sexual advances towards him. He was accused of attempted rape and was thrown into a cold, dark prison for two years. What have others put upon you that does not belong to you? What expectations are you forced to fulfil that diminish who you are? It's time to decide to stop being hidden or defined by other people's expectations of your life.

During these times of loneliness and isolation, God's favour and provision were with him. Others saw something in him that no one else had. It seemed no matter where he was, he was placed into positions of importance that required his influence, skills and sound judgement. When he was in prison, he was in charge of the other prisoners. When he was in Potiphar's house, he was the supervisor over all the other servants and, when he interpreted Pharaoh's dream, he became second in command over all of Egypt.

THREE DREAMS INTERPRETED:

Whilst Joseph was in prison, his anointing or favour on his life was evident and was repeatedly challenged. He had the opportunity to put into practice his gift of interpretation. He was in prison with two other men, who had been put into prison by Pharaoh. On one particular night, the cupbearer and the baker both had a dream, and Joseph was able to interpret each for them and they came to pass. The Cupbearer had been restored to serving Pharaoh, and the baker lost his life. It was another two years before the cupbearer remembered what Joseph had done for him, but it was the right time, because Pharaoh had two dreams and no one could interpret them.

So Joseph was called out of prison for the last time! I don't want to skip over this part: he came out of prison for the last time! Pharaoh, the ruler, had two dreams, where he saw seven fat cows that then became lean, and seven grains that were fat and then lean. Joseph's wisdom came into play, where he encouraged Pharaoh to put a man in charge of a national food bank to save grain for seven years to cover the seven years of famine. I've talked about famine in detail in the previous chapter, and you can revisit the action steps to identify any areas of famine.

There is a time for everything so, when we look at our lives, there is a purpose for it, even amidst our pain. God has a manual or a purpose for our lives. For example, when you purchase a car or electrical product, there are normally some instructions on how you should take care of it and use it, so what it was intended for is fulfilled and used for its best results. For instance, a manual may say:

- Do not store under 30°c
- Do not expose to light
- Do not drop in water
- Keep away from children

I discuss misuse and abuse in more detail in **Chapter Nineteen**. What would happen if we did what the manufacturer told us to do?

SEEING THROUGH THE EYES OF PURPOSE

- The item would work as it was supposed to.
- There would be fewer breakdowns.
- It would work to its full capacity.
- The item would last longer.
- You would get the full benefit out of the product.

So, looking at your life, you can consider that there are certain principles to identify your purpose or destiny and, in my opinion, there are five key factors to consider. These are listed in the 'action steps' section.

Some other key methods will help you grow in the area you are passionate about and want to develop. Write down the things you want to see in your life. Are you reading more books on your topic of interest? Are you reading books on leadership or motivation? Are you taking more time to spend with God in prayer, meditation, intermittent fasting and reading the Bible?

Are you saying Yes or No to the right things? Are you giving yourself time to do new fun activities? And finally, are you taking better care of yourself? So let's look at some action steps that will help you create a working map towards the part of the journey that helps you in identifying your purpose.

ACTION STEPS

1. What are you naturally attracted to?
   _____
   _____
   _____
   _____

2. What causes you the most pain? E.g people suffering, hunger, debt?
   _____
   _____
   _____
   _____

3. What groups of people do you identify with?
   _____
   _____
   _____
   _____

4. How do you show your empathy?
   _____
   _____
   _____
   _____

5. What do you want to see resolved?
   _____
   _____

SEEING THROUGH THE EYES OF PURPOSE

_____
_____

6. What can you start doing now to change?

_____
_____
_____
_____

PATHWAYS TO HEALING:
Overcoming Childhood Trauma and Adult Pain of Sibling Estrangement

CHAPTER SIXTEEN:
SUM OF THREE PARTS

As I've said earlier, we are the sum of three parts: body, soul, and spirit. If one area in your life is uncared for, for whatever reason, you will have an imbalance in your life. And this, in turn, will affect every aspect of your life. Think of it as a stool with three legs for support. If one of the supports falls off or breaks, the stool will be unbalanced and therefore unsuitable for use. That's how it is with our lives, as well.

If there's a problem with one aspect of our life, it affects other areas. It shows up in many different ways: through our negative attitude or how it affects our self-esteem. We begin to question our status and self-negating thoughts begin to develop. Feelings of blame and shame come soon after, and it won't matter whether a situation has placed us in this emotional state; this will just become our default way of thinking.

An imbalanced life will bring about a massive change in our emotions and attitude. That's not all - our physiological state will also be affected. The trauma will cause us to be sick because it is deeply rooted in our subconscious. All of these negative feelings cause stagnation and prevent progress in life.

PATHWAYS TO HEALING:
Overcoming Childhood Trauma and Adult Pain of Sibling Estrangement

Our self-esteem will also be negatively affected—it lies to you and tells you that you're not good enough. It will make you believe something is wrong with you and, as such, you're not lovable. Depression and the internal dialogue we have with fear that leads to mental health issues have become a big issue in our society today. We discuss Depression in more detail in **Chapter Seventeen.**

To get over this feeling, we have to find someone who has the professional ability to support us with whom we can share our fears. We must be ready to let this person help us unpack the layers of our deepest fears, so they can help us overcome the trauma we're dealing with. If you cannot find someone with whom you feel completely comfortable, try to find a community group that will help with this kind of situation. There are a lot of them around; some are even online. Better still, you can contact your local church.

It's hard to seek help, I know, but I hope you can seek the support that will help you heal. Getting your life back is going to start with a decision - I think you're getting the point by now! If you don't decide to regain control of your life, you'll just remain in the state you're in now. Remember that all things in life began by making a decision, consciously or otherwise. The scripture says: *"Before I formed you in the womb, I knew you before you were born, I set you apart..."* – Jeremiah 1:5[(NIV)].

SUM OF THREE PARTS

You are wonderfully made, you are loved, you are special, and you are unique. Because our experiences and feelings change with time, they are not enough to rely on. We need to look at the truth about who we are. So today, a different decision can be made; that it's time to lay aside all the negativity and start believing the truth about who you are. Is today your day, or maybe tomorrow, when you start to believe in yourself and that your life is worth it? Then, reach out for the right kind of support.

When we think about the issues surrounding **sibling** interaction, we tend to all have had experiences that made us feel good at the time. It made us feel happy and hopeful about a good life together. But unfortunately, sometimes, the pain we go through and feel is ignored most of the time and can outweigh the happiness, making us feel down too often. However, if the level of stress heightens, it can amplify several other issues that may include some of the things already mentioned in this book.

You might have experienced some of these feelings for a while and didn't know you were going through them at a high level of stress or mental imbalance. It can also come through your experience of grief when you lose someone you love and you can't seem to get over it. Grief comes in different ways, not just through physical death, but also a loss of a friendship, a marriage, job loss, or a separation from your children.

PATHWAYS TO HEALING:
Overcoming Childhood Trauma and Adult Pain of Sibling Estrangement

Most people do not admit to feeling depressed. They often cover it up with generic responses because they want to appear fine. For example, when someone asks, "How are you?", most of the time our response will be "I'm fine" when, in actuality, we are not.

'Fine' is now used to mean something completely different; it has now been socially accepted as defining an insurmountable number of emotions in one statement. **Fine** is not an emotion. According to one of the definitions, the meaning is "of very high quality; very good of its kind" (Oxford Dictionaries online). So, when someone asks how we are, we don't say I am "very good of its kind."

We have accepted the phrase 'I'm fine' to incorporate a totality of our emotions. We've identified it as a testament to how we feel at a particular moment in time–whether sadness, fear, loneliness or feeling isolated. It has become an accepted word to define our feelings, without having to say, I am feeling depressed, or I am feeling sad. It's important to note that these feelings do not necessarily mean we are suffering from depression. We talk about this in more detail in the next chapter.

So, now that you have been able to identify where you are, it makes it much easier for you to know which direction to take next through the maze. In the next chapter, we will continue to unravel those things that have kept you stuck, and get you to a place where you can start living your best life.

PATHWAYS TO HEALING:
Overcoming Childhood Trauma and Adult Pain of Sibling Estrangement

CHAPTER SEVENTEEN:
DEPRESSION

According to rethink.org, depression episodes are not all the same. They manifest in many different and diverse ways. However, what is generally agreed on is that depression causes an unenthusiastic feeling towards one's life that can be very unhealthy. Usually, this feeling doesn't go away and can last for a long time. If we have low moods over a long period, it's an indicator if we are just sad or depressed, and we may have other regular episodes, like staying in bed, not taking care of ourselves, isolation and having low energy. One example is sadness.

Usually, a person is sad because they are dissatisfied with current events. Normally, the sad person will bounce back onto their feet in a couple of days. And, even in their sad state of mind, they can still pick themselves up and do things effectively.

Unfortunately, depression comes into our lives and we start to change into different people. If you have experienced being a depressed person, can you relate to having no interest in your life or in the lives of others? Did you tend to isolate yourself more from your family and you didn't want to interact with others and it became minimal over time? This can usually go on for years for some and, without seeking help, the results can be devastating. People who identify with being depressed tend to always have a low mood, which affects their ability to be actively involved in daily activities. These phenomena will not be new to you if you've gone through the pain that has caused you to lose your identity. I know now that I was depressed on and off for so many years and did not realise it. It's been more than just feeling sad but I didn't know I was depressed. I didn't seek any professional help for it, as I hadn't been taught how to deal with my feelings. So I became a person who was introverted, shy, who lacked confidence and any zeal for life. It says in Proverbs 12:25 (ESV) – *'Anxiety in a man's heart weighs him down, but a good word makes him glad.'*

Here are a few quick notes on depression to help you understand it better:

DEPRESSION IS:

- a mental illness that is recognised worldwide
- common and affects about one in ten people
- something that anyone can get
- treatable

DEPRESSION IS NOT:

- something you can just 'snap out of'
- a sign of weakness.
- something that everyone experiences.

HOW COMMON IS DEPRESSION?

This is nothing new to any of us. We live in a world that at times makes us experience some pains and even mental health issues, because we have had no relief from what we've gone through. Depression is very common across the globe. It doesn't matter how old you are, or what your ethnic or cultural background is or even your status. It can affect people from all walks of life, including children. Experts predict that about one in ten people will be diagnosed with depression at least once in their lifetime. The truth is, there is no accurate way to know the true rate of this prediction, so the numbers may even be higher than this. However, research has shown that women are more likely than men to be dealing with one form of mental issue or another. This includes feelings of sadness, fear, the insecurity that comes with their physical appearance, just to mention a few. I have expressed earlier that wherever you experience the most pain will often have the greatest impact on your daily life. Let's say that you're a very emotional person, or you're fairly spiritual, and your source of pain comes from any of these areas, then it'll affect all other aspects of your life.

This includes how you act, your decision-making process, your interaction with others, and how you feel about yourself. This is why it is important to try and maintain a good balance in every aspect of your life.

If you've experienced the darkness of depression, it can be hard to seek help and bring light into your situation, and it can be hard to believe that you can be happy. So, let's take another step forward by doing some more action steps through the maze of your journey. Also in the next chapter, we will be looking at some more Plan of Action activities you can take to help you even further.

ACTION STEPS

Your Most Dominant Focus

1. Which is the most dominant area in your life that you focus on the most (e.g. physical, spiritual or emotional)?

   _____
   _____
   _____
   _____

2. Have you ever felt depressed? If so, for how long?

   _____
   _____
   _____
   _____

3. What clues have you seen in your experiences that you think can lead you to your greatest victory? (Are you an empath, caring or an encourager)?

   _____
   _____
   _____
   _____

PATHWAYS TO HEALING:
Overcoming Childhood Trauma and Adult Pain of Sibling Estrangement

CHAPTER EIGHTEEN:
PLAN OF ACTION

If you've felt like the way you used to live your life has put you at a disadvantage, and you've been trying to get back on track without success, I'll suggest what you can consider as an option to deal with it. In this kind of situation, the key is to identify the problem and work towards regaining control of your life by having a plan. See, what many seem to take for granted is the fact that we let too many things control how we live. This happens to people who just live their lives without a specific plan of action.

Living this way allows us to be open and vulnerable to the whims of others, and to be impulsive of things that we cannot even control. And when we do this, we enable external forces to prevent us from moving forward. Then we end up saying things like, "If my mum hadn't left me, I would be so much further on in my life," or "If my dad had told me he loved me, I wouldn't be so hurt inside." These are all valid feelings, and we start to blame everything and everyone else but ourselves for our stagnation. While having a sense of belonging and our parents' love is the key to healthy development, this shouldn't be what defines our future experiences, although I know the impact of not having this can be devastating. The fact that your parents didn't show you love, or the fact that some students in your school constantly picked on you, shouldn't stop you from achieving something worthwhile. Try looking at it from a different perspective; for instance, at least you saw your parents and went to school. There are millions of children who don't even know who their parents are. There are many children in foster homes jumping from one family to the next. Yet, many of them turn out great. So, what you have experienced in your life shouldn't stop you from doing great things. The Bible reaffirms to us that we are more than conquerors, so we need to start believing what the truth says about us, and look for our confidence to be increased.

When you allow external factors to affect you to this extent, especially things that happened in the past, it becomes your reality. In other words, it becomes your norm. And that which seems to be our norm is a reflection of our experiences and the things that have happened to us. What we then say to ourselves and what others have said to us will continue to echo in our heads like a foghorn. This will reproduce itself in every aspect of our body, soul and spirit. As mentioned before, all forms of trauma can affect us in several immeasurable ways. The effect of traumatic experiences manifests in our behaviour. This includes our relationships, how we treat others and feel about ourselves, and our interpretation of the world around us. Often, this tends to get us into trouble in certain situations where our traumatic experience makes us behave negatively. Instead of being apologetic, we try to defend our actions, and that is not healthy. Traumatic experiences leave a significant imprint on our personality and it takes time to root out its effects, but we can't do it alone; we do need help.

A classic example of this is when you experience the effects of a broken relationship. This is something we have all experienced. Your relationships could have fallen apart because of what you did, or it could be the other person's fault. No matter whose fault it was, broken relationships usually leave a sour taste in your mouth. You start to feel uncomfortable with your life, further distorting how we view other relationships in the future. In one moment, everything in your life is going well, and then, all of a sudden, or gradually, what was once a non-issue starts to cause problems. Your circle of friends begins to feel offended and jealous. Then you gain awareness that this has brought about a massive change, turning your life upside down.

The unexpected, and sometimes unrecognisable, ways people treat us now seem to be taking a different turn. In this kind of situation, we've allowed a previous bad experience to dictate how we react to similar and future events. We've become so familiar with the hurt that we don't realise how it is affecting every relationship and that it's causing us to live a disjointed life. We begin to live a life devoid of joy, peace, and stability. A situation like this isn't unique to failed relationships alone. It could be a host of many other things, such as the unfair treatment we experienced in the workplace. It could also be the many sly and uncomfortable comments and instances when you have been mocked. There are some people whose intention is only to hurt you; they want to get a reaction because, strangely, they enjoy it. It's easy to believe that we are only arguing or fighting with the person(s) standing right in front of us, and that is true to some extent. We feel the sting of their harsh words, they pierce us deeply and we see the rage in their eyes.

However, the Bible reminds us that we're in a spiritual battle that requires us to wear spiritual armour that covers us, ready for the battle. We're told in. -Ephesians 6:10-18$^{(NIV)}$ to *"Finally, be strong in the Lord and in his mighty power. ^{11} Put on the full armour of God, so that you can take your stand against the devil's schemes. ^{12} For our struggle is not against flesh and blood, but against the rulers, against the authorities, against the powers of this dark world and against the spiritual forces of evil in the heavenly realms. ^{13} Therefore put on the full armour of God, so that when the day of evil comes, you may be able to stand your ground, and after you have done everything, to stand. Stand firm then, with the belt of truth buckled around your waist, with the breastplate of righteousness in place, ^{15} and with your feet fitted with the readiness that comes from the gospel of peace. ^{16} In addition to all this, take up the shield of faith, with which you can extinguish all the flaming arrows of the evil one. ^{17} Take the helmet of salvation and the sword of the Spirit, which is the word of God.*

PLAN OF ACTION

This armour is naked to the human eye, but we put it on by faith. This armour protects every area of our body, as mentioned above; the only area uncovered is our back, and in my understanding, the reason why the back is not covered is that there's no retreat for a soldier or fighter. And also God has our back covered. So I want to encourage you as we partner with God, and entrust Him with our lives to protect us and guide us.

Any negative words directed towards you, and any toxic experiences you have gone through, may have left you feeling like you've been hit by a truck. The wounds that form afterwards are usually very deep and difficult to live with, and we walk around with open wounds. But one thing you should realise is that these wounds bring some of the greatest and most significant lessons in our lives. Many times we fail to understand why we are going through these experiences. At times we will lash out at others because we're hurting. At times, how we treat people can be hurtful, too.

This may not be intentional, but sometimes it won't matter because our actions at times will be misunderstood and misinterpreted by some of those around us all the time. We must understand that other people also have experiences that have shaped them, and which have caused them to perceive things differently from us. So, you both have your side of the story until you come to the truth. We all need to learn how to communicate in such a way that others will understand us clearly. To do this right, we need to first understand and communicate with ourselves. Some of our biggest life lessons come from our closest relationships, and some of the deepest wounds we could ever experience also come from this same group of people. I think you get this now. We continue to take out our frustrations on those around us, and the cycle will continue to be perpetuated until someone says, "I'm not putting up with this anymore."

ENOUGH IS ENOUGH!

So, it's important to have friends in your life who are willing to call you out and set you right when you are going down the wrong path. Friends ultimately care so much about you and don't want you to stay as you are, so they tell you the truth in love. They're better off than those who pretend to be your friends but are your enemies. All they do is flatter you with their kisses and control you for their gain. They won't help you grow or change, nor will they wish for any positivity for you, because they want to keep controlling you.

Positive criticism is not always good or welcoming to the ear but, if you want to change and become a better person, it won't matter how many criticisms you get, as long as they impact your life for the better.

CHAPTER NINETEEN:
WEIGHTS & BAGGAGE

Can you imagine carrying around bags that weigh fifty pounds all day? You're carrying twenty-five pounds in each hand, and there is no time in the day when you can put them down, so when you come home, you're still drained and strained, both physically and mentally. You still want to put them down, but you just can't seem to let them go or find anywhere to place them. You want to feel light and be free to do other things that bring you joy; you want to feel more comfortable in the skin you're in. Aside from feeling the strain in every muscle in your body, it has now also inhibited your thinking, and ability to reason and make sound decisions.

Now, this is a typical representation of someone carrying emotional baggage. Imbalanced emotions can be heavy loads, and denying them doesn't make them disappear. When it's time to enjoy a good night's sleep, your muscles will tell you otherwise. Suppressing or masking the realities of your emotional baggage just makes you continue to carry the weight that affects you negatively. Our emotions are this unseen load, the ones we only see in our thoughts and behaviour. Often, we live our lives carrying more than one unseen baggage that weighs us down as time passes. Because of the significance of the several pieces of baggage we carry, we're unable to set our minds on a productive endeavour. Our conscious and subconscious states of mind eschew and regurgitate these thoughts repeatedly, making us live in a perpetual state of fear and agony. How much of your time and energy are taken up with negative issues? How much time have you spent looking at the past and feeling guilty over things that have happened? All plants start from seeds. For a seed to grow, it must be buried into the earth. It has to be hidden under the soil, where different chemical activities will take place for it to yield a harvest. Throughout this process, water and sunlight provide the nutrition and energy needed for it to grow. Without these two components, the plant will not survive. With the right combination and amount, however, it will flourish. Just like seeds, small issues can grow into big problems over time. That is why it's helpful to check out for problems that can disrupt the momentum of your life and uproot them while they're still small. The moment it becomes a big problem, it might become much more difficult to handle.

God loves us so much that He always wants us to see ourselves the way He sees us. He sees us as special and capable of doing anything, because He has created us without limiting our abilities. In the book of Genesis, the Bible tells us that He created us in His image and likeness. The problem is that we only see ourselves through the lens of our life's experiences. We define ourselves in terms of our successes and failures.

Unfortunately, this blurs our perception of life. In God's eyes, our uniqueness doesn't diminish, irrespective of what successes or failures we've come across. This is the only way we should always see ourselves: the way God sees us. It is only when you see you're exceptional that you will start to be strengthened. I know it will take time to start seeing yourself in a better light; you can then begin to face your problem confidently and assuredly. If you don't face it, it will continue tormenting you.

I am not saying this will be easy. Oh, it won't be easy – especially for someone who has wallowed in so much self-pain and low self-esteem. I would like you to start believing that you can have a better life and better experiences. It's when you decide to acknowledge that things are not as they should be that you can start moving forward with your life again. Don't look at the difficulty; instead, see the rewards after the challenging times are over. If you believe, you will overcome it. Let me use this analogy to describe it: pain can be like chewing gum. When you look at the basic ingredients of gum, it includes a gum base, softeners, sweeteners and flavourings. In its basic form, the gum is a kind of synthetic rubber.

This rubber, whether natural or artificial, is sensitive to temperature. What determines its flexibility is the amount of movement and saliva in your mouth, which keeps it soft so you can keep chewing it. So, the more you chew, the softer it gets. Just as gum sticks to every part of our mouth, so does pain

PATHWAYS TO HEALING:
Overcoming Childhood Trauma and Adult Pain of Sibling Estrangement

in every part of our lives. It makes things messy and tangled up, preventing you from making meaningful progress. Pain makes it impossible for you to see anything good for yourself, and puts you in a situation where you lose hope completely.

The things you give more energy and attention to are the things that determine how you live your life. So, what you chew over and over again in your mind and heart becomes the totality of your soul. The things you allow to stay active in your life will determine how active your life will be. Proverbs 23:7 (NIV) says, 'For as he thinketh in his heart, so is he.' Let's get back to the analogy. When gum sticks to our shoe, we apply a process to remove the gum. Our ability to walk conveniently depends entirely on the effectiveness of this process. That's similar to how we deal with pain. Without getting to the root of the issues that brought us pain, they will start to stick to our hearts and consume our lives from the inside out. They will start to affect our perception, and our hearts will begin to harden - metaphorically speaking - just like gum, when it's left to dry up.

There's a promise in Ezekiel 36:26 (NIV) - *"I will give you a new heart and put a new spirit in you; I will remove from you your heart of stone and give you a heart of flesh."* You can move through the healing process and, if anyone hurts you again, it won't affect you as deeply as before, because you will have learnt how to protect and guard your heart. Now is the time to welcome your healing, whether you have experienced verbal, physical, emotional, sexual or even spiritual abuse. It's a decision you make for yourself; you take your pain and use it as fuel to propel you forward towards a better life.

The Free Dictionary defines ABUSE in the following ways:

- To use improperly or excessively; misuse; abuse alcohol; abuse a privilege

- To hurt or injure by maltreatment; ill-use

- To force sexual activity on; rape or molest

- To assail with insulting or hurtful words

If you think it's time to let go of carrying around the weights of your emotions and for your pain to stop, then read on. It all starts with deciding to stop tolerating improper behaviour towards you. It's setting out boundaries on things you will no longer tolerate. I will suggest you look at the series of books by Dr Henry Cloud on boundaries, which will help you start setting up healthy boundaries in your life and relationships. So, after a nervous and maybe fearful decision is made, miraculously things begin to happen, and the universe begins to provide you with all you need to succeed. Pathways to Healing can be a journey taken by all of us at some point. Whenever someone is ready to change, it always seems as if things start to get worse. We can't take any more pain, trauma, famine or depression. We can't take any more self-hate... We just can't! I understand, and I hear you. I understand what you are going through. My friend, it's time to start allowing yourself to experience a brighter future. Seek help from those who can help you to heal. It's time to look deep down into your heart, and see that you deserve nothing short of the best.

It's time to love again, and time to believe again. It's time to know that you can be free to love, accept the good things in your life and be happy. So, let's take another step together by doing some action steps through the maze that will help you identify the things that are still sticking to you.

ACTION STEPS

What's Your Gum?

1. What things are continuing to stay flexible in your life, and are still binding you to all sorts of issues that you no longer want?

   _____
   _____
   _____
   _____

2. Let's celebrate how far you have come. List the changes that have already taken place in you or the situations that have positively impacted you so far.

   _____
   _____
   _____
   _____

3. What new experiences do you want in your life that will make you a more balanced person?

   _____
   _____
   _____
   _____

PATHWAYS TO HEALING:
Overcoming Childhood Trauma and Adult Pain of Sibling Estrangement

CHAPTER TWENTY:
YOU ARE UNIQUE

Do you know how special and unique you are? I know you must have heard this so many times before that it almost sounds like a cliché. You've heard it so much it doesn't strike any chord in you anymore, or maybe you've never heard it. But hey, I'm telling you that you're special. The only thing that will make this false is if God isn't real. You're a mirror image of God. How are you anything but unique? I know that your experiences may have caused you to start thinking of yourself as irrelevant. They have you thinking you don't matter. Hey, you do! Irrespective of what you've gone through in life, you're nothing but unique, and you'll remain so until God stops saying so, which is not possible! Because of this, your story will have an amazing conclusion.

You've gone through a lot of things some people wouldn't have been able to go through, so let's just stop here, celebrate and break out into dancing! This is why you will end up being a success in life. Know that your experiences are not a totality of your life, and you can begin a new chapter. You can rewrite it by:

PATHWAYS TO HEALING:
Overcoming Childhood Trauma and Adult Pain of Sibling Estrangement

- Loving you again.

- Accepting and liking yourself—flaws and all.

- Creating a happy now and future on your terms.

- Being restored to a place of honour.

- Having people in your life that appreciate and love you.

- Gaining the ability to say yes or no, without needing to explain yourself.

I imagine you have come to a point in your life where you are already having this conversation with yourself. I also imagine that you are saying Yes because something has to change! I congratulate you as you've already started on your path to healing; I'm so excited for you! If you have decided that you're hungry for a turnaround in your life - in your family and your relationships - then I hope that seeing the bigger picture of your life will show your purpose.

Need I remind you again, that God has a plan: *"For I know the plans I have for you,' declares the Lord, 'plans to prosper you and not to harm you, plans to give you hope and a future"* – Jeremiah 29:11 [NIV]

God is good! At times, bad things do and will happen in your life. Yet God has never stopped loving and accepting you through all of what you have gone through. Yes, all of it. He is able and willing to bring you to a place of freedom, hope, and change. So, always remember you can overcome anything. You are a winner. When you have experienced some form of sibling rejection, you tend not to see what comes after the pain and heartache. There's a desire to see everything in our lives positively: better opportunities, better friendships, better influence, and a better family. If these are our thoughts for ourselves, then imagine how much more His plans are for us, and what He has given us control over.

The cost of greatness is always high, and I know you've felt you have no more to pay, but there are no shortcuts to get to this stage in your life. When we undergo difficult situations in our lives, we do not see the circumstances as a learning experience. All we want is to get out of it.

For me to be able to hold onto hope when there was no hope, I held onto the middle. The middle, you say? Yes, the middle of His will. When you're in the middle of something, you've gone so far ahead that you can't even think of going back. What would you be going back for, anyway? So, may I suggest you reach out and continue to walk to the end of the maze of your pain? Please keep on moving forward with the support you need. The cost is always high. But just you and God know the price that was paid for your greatness to come to the forefront. God paid a great price as well to restore you to wholeness and a relationship with Him. He does not ask us to do something He has not already done. For instance, His high price was the gift of His Son, Jesus, to be a holy sacrifice given for your pain, hurt, rejection, sadness, and He offers you a restored life. He loves you that much! We can't get our head around it; it's a wonderful gift just for you to accept. This was reflected in John 10:10 (NIV) – *"The thief comes only to steal and kill and destroy; I have come that they may have life, and have it to the full."*

The power I talk about is not endured; it's given to you from Him. During my restoration and healing, I was sick for two years and, on and off, several strange things started showing up in my body. Was my body lying to me? What was my body telling me? What was I missing? My point here is that we need to listen to our body when it is telling us something is not right. Our body speaks a language and we must learn to understand it. When the body is stressed, it signals you in many ways. So, you should find time to rest and allow your body to heal from the inside out. Listening to soothing music, praying, and meditating, is a good start. I hope by now you hear my heart. The word of God can reveal truths to you about both who you are and your circumstances. You can turn your situation around, and change the negative thoughts by thinking about the truth of your situation. Then, you can get back to a place where you are free to feel empowered in your voice, so you can sing out loud! But it's hard to sing when you have no words. Even in the quiet, though, God hears and understands your silence, as it speaks volumes to Him. He wants you to get to the place in your life where your confidence in Him is so strong that you're not affected by your past.

This is so you're not influenced by the expectations of people who want to control you. And you're not swayed by what people do, what they say, what they don't do, and what they don't say. God wants you to know that He validates you; He accepts you just as you are. He wants you to be free from people and circumstances that get in the way of your relationship with Him. Occasionally, we might not understand His timing because His process seems to take a long time in our eyes.

But He sees the end before the beginning, and He wants to purify and cleanse our heart, so it's supple enough for us to change and receive all the good things He wants to pour into it. God already knows the end. In the next action steps, we will look at the level of your love tank—is it empty or half full?

ACTION STEPS

Your Love Tank

1. How much joy is in your life? Do you like your own company?

   _____
   _____
   _____
   _____

2. What makes you smile or burst out laughing?

   _____
   _____
   _____
   _____

3. What can you do to bring more joy to your life?

   _____
   _____
   _____
   _____

4. When will you start to make some positive changes/and what will these be? (add a date to these tasks)

   _____
   _____
   _____
   _____

CHAPTER TWENTY – ONE:
IT'S WORKING FOR YOUR GOOD

After several doctors and hospital visits, the doctors could not find any medical evidence to support my symptoms. Although a few years later I did suffer from a condition called labyrinthitis, I woke up one morning and the first thing on my mind was about the family issues I'd been going through and, within minutes, I just heard a pop in my head. And I remember when I tried to lift my head, it was limp, and it just fell back onto the bed. At the time, I called to my husband and told him to pray. I was able to lift my head after that, but I did not feel good. The crazy thing was that I went to work! If you've ever experienced having vertigo, it's similar to that. It's all connected to the inner ear and balance.

So when I was walking, I would lose my balance and almost have a floating bounce in my step. If I was going to have an episode – which would feel like my head was falling forward - I could not feel the ground beneath me; it was horrible. Also, when I would try to lay my head down and then try to raise it, my head would start spinning, and I would have to hold my head with both hands and place my head back onto the

PATHWAYS TO HEALING:
Overcoming Childhood Trauma and Adult Pain of Sibling Estrangement

pillow and wait for the spinning to stop. In about two years, I did eventually get over this, thank God, but boy, it was hard to go through. I didn't know what this was all about until I was introduced to the ministry of Katie Souza, which I found to be an eye-opener. Her ministry focuses on the healing of the soul, from any experience that may have caused us trauma at any stage in our life, or that may be a generational issue. We know that trauma shows up in so many different ways - be it sickness, a lack of joy, anger, unforgiveness or disappointment.

Her ministry is all about educating people on the importance of Soul health so that we can be free from these negative cycles and start living a happier and victorious life. It was then I realised that my soul - my will, mind and emotions - were screaming out loudly for help. But, as I had no point of reference, I did not recognise their voices or notice the silent stirring of my soul—the pain had become me, and I was not aware of it. I was focusing on the pain and could not see myself anymore! All the issues I was experiencing were in my tissues, and they were affecting my life in many ways that I couldn't comprehend. They affected me terribly. I was turning into a completely different person. It was so bad I could hardly recognise myself. Can you identify with this? Have you been lost in your pains?

I was no longer smiling and my life was becoming dull. My soul needed to heal from the years of pain, bitterness, hurt and blame it had gone through. It was eating me alive. My pains were a daily open wound that was not healing. Bitterness encourages negative emotions to fester, allowing bad influences to affect you, the only purpose being to make us feel miserable and not to thrive. This leads to anger, giving room for bad things to happen. That may sound scary; no-one wants to be living his or her life like that.

There will always be times when, while communicating with others, you will be misunderstood. When someone tells a lie about you or misrepresents you, and they do not apologise or retract the lie, you will feel upset, and the lie is out there, growing, and there is nothing you can do about it because it's now gone far and wide. But we need to go through the process of letting go. The journey towards total recovery is taken one step at a time. And remember, you can walk this walk like the many before you and the many that will come after you. However, the question remains: how can you heal something you can't see? You decide to allow the grace of God to help you. The common definition describes God's grace as 'the unmerited favour of God toward man' (BillyGraham.org). Unmerited favour means gaining approval, acceptance, special benefits or blessings. This sounds good to me, what say you? I learned that, over time, God indeed wanted me to be healed in the deepest places of my soul, so that I had to trust that only He could reach those places, and then allow Him to gently remove all the things I no longer needed or wanted.

PATHWAYS TO HEALING:
Overcoming Childhood Trauma and Adult Pain of Sibling Estrangement

There will be times when your hope seems so far away that you wonder, "What is the point?" I know that, even if you think you have lost it all, there is a point. But remember what was said before, that nothing you've gone through will be wasted.

It will all work out in your favour. Nothing, not one issue, not one embarrassing moment, not one hurtful experience will go without benefitting you in the end. In experiencing sibling rejection and estrangement, I found there has to be a moment of grace that you give yourself.

You are worth saving; you deserve forgiveness and self-love. Also, let yourself express this grace to others, irrespective of what you're going through. I know this is hard, but you don't want to be angry forever, do you? The cost is far too high. It's time for you to move forward on the path of healing. You might be in the toughest position in your life right now, but just wake up every day appreciating seeing another day, whereby you are closer to your breakthrough than you were yesterday. God is helping you to get closer to your destination in life.

For some, the breakthrough has an impact on how the body handles what it is going through. The mind is a wonderful thing, and we must be careful of what we dwell on. The mind is the root of all conscious and subconscious thoughts. So, anything you encounter will remain within you, even if you cannot recall it. These things can go on to affect our lives without us knowing it. Psychologists confirm this much. That is why we must be careful with our self-talk.

In time, what is weighing you down will have to come out. It can be through talking with someone, praying, taking up journaling or going for counselling. Everyone has a unique healing process, and you'll surely find yours. We were not built to carry so much stressful mental weight. It all has to come out. We were not built to carry so much hurt, anger or disappointment. We were made for LOVE—remember that. You can find your way back to LOVE. It's our natural position, and we need to get back to our rightful place, so we can fulfil our purpose and destiny.

God knows what you've gone through, and He wants you to be well in your body and your soul. I know the pain can be too much, but remember, what we've gone through can work for our good. I don't know how He does it. He can use the broken pieces, the things we hide in the depths of our soul, and make us whole again. He can make it work for our good and His glory. So, let's look at the next action steps to identify any physical issues you may have experienced.

ACTION STEPS

Your Physical Body

1. Are you listening to your body? What has changed?

   _____
   _____
   _____
   _____

2. What suppressed issues are you not listening to (consider any changes in your body, and how you've been feeling)?

   _____
   _____
   _____
   _____

3. What can you do now to work towards becoming a healthier person (both emotionally and physically)?

   _____
   _____
   _____
   _____

CHAPTER TWENTY- TWO:
DEALING WITH REJECTION

Rejection causes huge emotional turmoil for any individual It can be so tragic, especially because it is something that is so subtle and can go totally unnoticed when it occurs. Rarely will you find people who will reject you to your face. No, most wouldn't, but some people are brazen and will. Some do it silently and behind your back. They pretend to like you when you come around but, as soon as you turn your back, that's it. I experienced this first-hand, and I must tell you it wasn't a good feeling. It was masked by other people's pretentious behaviour. The worst part is that you'll sense something isn't right with their reaction towards you, but you'll never really know what it is. You'll start to question yourself, and self-doubt will begin to set in because you will think you've done something wrong. It can almost drive you crazy. Can you relate to having a family member or a friend who always left you feeling somewhat unsettled?

Maybe after talking with them, you felt as if you've done something wrong, because the conversation didn't go the way you thought it should. You can swear something was out of place, but you aren't sure what it is. You struggle to put a finger on it. Sometimes, we dismiss this, even though it keeps bugging us. But what's the real issue? I mean, you sense there's an underlying problem, but you don't know its source. What can you do about it without knowing where it is coming from? The best thing is just to try and ignore it.

However, ignoring issues like these is the mistake we make. We must listen to our natural intuition when it speaks to us, because it is trying to reveal something important to us. We must never ignore our gut feeling, just because we cannot find a logical explanation for it. If you want to hear the truth, you need to listen to your senses and ask God to show you the truth, which is what I did. Weigh the situation up, so that you are not judging someone without having all the facts to hand. We don't always get it right, though—we suppress our inner voice because we cannot understand it. In this case, if we suppress this voice for too long, it will end up causing more problems than we bargained for. Dealing with rejection is a very delicate matter that, if you can, needs to be handled with sensitivity. This can be painful and may take some time, depending on your circumstances.

So, let's look at how to deal with rejection. We all go through difficult times in our life; mine was in trying to fit in with some of my family and friends. Feeling different is like a wave that washes over you, which you can never get free from. I would like to say now that I was special in my unique way, and this made me easily misunderstood.

DEALING WITH REJECTION

My upbringing had a major impact on my ability to trust others, particularly men. After going through relationships that were strained and full of insecurities, you realise you work hard to get people's approval and acceptance. In my case, even when I had got the approval, I would still be looking for it.

You experience rejection and abuse if:

- You've been talked down to, made to feel unimportant, or your opinions were ridiculed.

- You have been mocked.

- People gossip about you with others, behind your back, and pretend to be your friend.

- You were gaslighted – where others make you question your sanity and devalue your feelings and perception of a situation. Where you're left feeling confused and questioning your reality.

- You've been controlled and manipulated; you feel confused and start to not trust your perception and thoughts.

- The devaluation of your feelings and perception of a situation was undervalued.

When I was going through my difficult times, I didn't even know how to process it. I wasn't physically hurt, and that was the only way I thought a person could feel deep pain. It took many years before I knew emotional pain also existed. This kind of pain occurs when you have negative words and feelings directed at you, because that is how people have treated you for most of your life. This was the kind of treatment I was subjected to, and it destroyed my self-esteem. I lost my identity completely and all my self-confidence. Unconditional love from some of my family members was virtually non-existent.

It was so bad that I always thought I was the cause of the problem. At the time, I started to question whether my parents were my real parents. I had this notion in my head that I was adopted, because I couldn't understand how some of my family members would treat me so negatively. The feeling was that I wasn't welcome. But why would I be rejected? I didn't bring myself into this world…

These were the thoughts and questions that kept playing in my mind, which I couldn't understand. At a very tender age, I started becoming a troubled person. I would distance myself as a coping mechanism in an attempt to try to understand it all. I mentioned that I never knew the unconditional love of a dad, which had a major negative impact on my life for far too long. At times, when I think about it, it's almost impossible for me to believe I went through this. I found myself writing more poems, which I now have around sixty or more of. That was one way I could express myself since there was no one I could talk to about it. The Scriptures revealed to me that I was special to God. They reminded me that He chose me, and He accepts me as a daughter. This has brought me major relief and helped me to accept myself for who I am. Despite this, something always tried to deter me from believing this truth from God. These thoughts came in this form:

- Various people close to me had wrongly accused me of things I hadn't done - both minor and major issues - that did not warrant that much focus. It was all to discredit my character.

- I had been verbally and emotionally bullied for years, to my face or behind my back, with no basis of evidence. The difficulty of experiencing this is that a small lie is like a seed and it can grow into a bigger lie. It has deep roots, which can lead to the lie being mistaken as the truth. It can be hard to tear it down, because there are many other factors to a lie; it's like a spider's web, designed to catch others in its web of lies.

Those who have shared the lies, and the ones believing the lie, can get stuck in it themselves as well and can't seem to get free. The lie has many parts to it, feeding and festering. Emotional abuse becomes steeped in interactions involving those who continue to perpetuate the lie.

The use of manipulation, which controls how others see things, how they think and how they act, becomes crucial to maintaining the believability of the lie. This is because anyone involved in this mess has already been conditioned to perceive

PATHWAYS TO HEALING:
Overcoming Childhood Trauma and Adult Pain of Sibling Estrangement

you and the situation as the problem and the issue, the one to be hated. Are you getting this? So, where you are concerned, an unseen wall becomes erect, mixing the truths and lies into one big, messy pile. When they hear something about you, they will always believe it and do nothing to challenge the validity of the accusations. So, considering all that, we don't get stuck there.

Dealing with rejection starts with taking several steps towards focusing on your self-care. These are some suggestions; you can find some more listed in Chapter Twenty-Seven, Pathways to Healing, as well. So the first question I would like to ask you is, What do you do when you are alone? I know in those times when I'm alone I get closer to God. I've found that I just talk to my friend. I don't let my mouth do all the talking for me, but I let my heart do it, and I just let it all pour out! In those moments, I feel no judgement and no fear.

It's a place where I can be me, with my hurts, disappointments, aspirations and, most importantly, it's a place where I know I will not be rejected! For some people, being alone is a scary place. It can be a place where a lot of the issues that they have suppressed can come up, which they are not yet ready to face. Some people cope by having the radio on 24/7 throughout the day, or they like being around people all the time – so they never have any time to themselves to think and because they just can't deal with their issues!

DEALING WITH REJECTION

So another step you can implement is if you've been invited to a gathering, where you know those who treat you disrespectfully may be present—and you know the outcome is always the same—you can get back to the person who invited you and decline the invitation by saying "Sorry, but no, I can't make it" without any long explanation, as No is a complete sentence. Equally, if you do decide to go, once you are there you can remove yourself from the crowd to protect yourself. Remember, you can't isolate yourself from every social gathering, but it is your choice to start building up your confidence and creating new boundaries for your self-care. You can continue to start making healthy decisions for yourself, you stand up for yourself, even when no one else does.

You start to honour yourself. Remember, you start believing the truth about who you are: your uniqueness, that you are special, and you are more precious than gold.

So let's look a bit closer at your own experience in the next set of action steps.

PATHWAYS TO HEALING:
Overcoming Childhood Trauma and Adult Pain of Sibling Estrangement

ACTION STEPS

Your Experience

1. Can you identify those people who have caused you the most pain in your life?

   _____
   _____
   _____
   _____

2. How did they treat you?

   _____
   _____
   _____
   _____

3. How did it make you feel?

   _____
   _____
   _____
   _____

4. List whom you need to forgive (Remember, forgiveness sets you free)

   _____
   _____
   _____
   _____

DEALING WITH REJECTION

5. How are you feeling now? Find replacements for negative words e.g. "I feel hate" for "I feel love".

   _____
   _____
   _____
   _____

PATHWAYS TO HEALING:
Overcoming Childhood Trauma and Adult Pain of Sibling Estrangement

CHAPTER TWENTY-THREE:
THIS SQUARE PEG DOES NOT FIT

At this point in your life, you may have had so many mixed experiences - too many to count. There would have been misunderstandings, some lies, and yes, plenty of smiles. Now that you are enthusiastic about regaining control over your life, it's important to seek grace for yourself and for others. Be mindful that, at this point, there is a tendency for pride to set in.

The wrong kind of pride can lead a person to see themselves as superior over others, which can be damaging to any relationship. However, with the right type of pride, you can lead an appreciative life—further offsetting the shame you've been living with for so long. The Bible mentions the word 'shame' over four hundred and thirty-one times. It also describes the consequences of its existence in one's life. God sees you in your daily dealings, and has taken away your shame. He can relate to our experience of shame. *'He was despised and rejected by mankind, a man of suffering, and familiar with pain.'* – Isaiah 53:3 [NIV].

PATHWAYS TO HEALING:
Overcoming Childhood Trauma and Adult Pain of Sibling Estrangement

One thing peculiar about pain is that when it becomes unbearable, it usually indicates that your breakthrough is around the corner. Therefore, you just have to hold out a little while longer and seek strength from God. Nothing comes easy, and your greatness is no different. It is then that you will realise all you've gone through - all the pain and ridicule you've faced has prepared you for your moment of greatness and freedom.

A passage in the Scriptures says, *'He will restore the years the cankerworm and locust have stolen.'* – Joel 2:25 (KJB). This is telling us that, with time, God will restore everything we have lost. It reassures us that God is with us, and He sees us as we struggle through our difficulties. In the end, He has plans to restore us to a good life. God understands how valuable time is for us as humans. He created it after all, so He knows that time is our life. He knows that it is our energy. In this passage, He declares that He will restore all the time that our pain has taken away, including everything that has taken our joy and happiness. Yes, I believe that everything is working for our good. These are not my words; you'll find them in the book of Romans 8:28 (NLT). There has to be a place where we can express gratitude in our lives, which is the complete opposite of what we've experienced—having gratitude for getting to this place in your life, for making it through. The opportunity to be grateful allows and makes room for more good and beautiful things to come into your life. This is to tell you the importance of showing gratitude to God by thanking Him. So, after you've got back your control for your life, never forget to show gratitude. When we are grateful, we activate Heaven to open up many more pleasant possibilities in our lives.

WHAT WAS JOSEPH FIGHTING AGAINST?

The coat his father, Jacob, gave him made him know that he was special and favoured. However, the rejection he experienced from his siblings was an invisible coat that he had to fight. The real fight was about his identity. It was about who he was, without the protection that came from his father's love. His identity and character were challenged at every step of his journey in exile. But in a quiet place, and with the stillness of time, God showed him who he was. We all desire to know who we are. Everyone will come to a time in their own lives when they will ask the question: Who am I? Joseph experienced so much in his life—events that happened concurrently. Looking at each incident demanded that another level of his character had to be developed, and it all started in his family:

- Not feeling like he was a part of his family - yet loved by his father.

- Being thrown into a pit by his brothers.

- Being sold to the Ishmaelites and taken to Egypt.

- Being accused of rape.

- Being thrown into prison.

- Being elevated into a leadership role.

- Facing and forgiving those who sold him into slavery.

All of what he went through affected him psychologically, emotionally and physically. So, let's take a look at where you are in the maze, and see where you are on your path. You're getting closer to your destination of healing. The next action steps will pinpoint how far you've come on this path.

ACTION STEPS

Your Journey

1. Where do you think you are on your journey right now?

   _____
   _____
   _____
   _____

2. What areas in your life do you feel you've overcome?

   _____
   _____
   _____
   _____

3. Where will you seek help? (through counselling, or talk to a friend)

   _____
   _____
   _____
   _____

4. What new things will you do now, towards your recovery?

   _____
   _____
   _____
   _____

PATHWAYS TO HEALING:
Overcoming Childhood Trauma and Adult Pain of Sibling Estrangement

CHAPTER TWENTY-FOUR:
RELATIONSHIP CHALLENGES

There are things we have gone through that almost break us and bring us to our knees. The fact you are still here shows that you can overcome anything, and that the future has more in store for you. Joseph had many strained relationships within his family, and every interaction he had with them affected how he saw himself, how he interacted with those around him, and the aspirations he had for his own life. Though he was chosen for this difficult experience, Joseph's story shows several challenges which, if anyone else went through them, they might not have come out the other side triumphantly:

- Joseph was placed in difficult situations.

- He dealt with people who hated and resented him.

- He was placed in a place of isolation for years.

- He had to become responsible for his own life.

We can be affected by negative energy and relationships that we have been involved in, or are still involved in. These bring challenges into our lives and can affect us in many areas, but

I will focus on just three. I think these are broken down into the three Ws. The 1st 'W' is: What challenges did Joseph face?, the 2nd 'W' is: Who was he going to forgive?, and the final 'W' is: What physical challenges did he experience?

1. WHAT CHALLENGES DID JOSEPH FACE?

Joseph was constantly challenged about what he believed. Reflecting on his story and your own, you can consider the following questions:

- What was the root cause of his anger?

- How high was the intensity of the pain and rejection he was feeling?

- How did he respond to these challenges?

- How was he able to help others, even when he was in pain?

Think about your own experiences and the numerous challenges you've faced, and how this has affected you psychologically. Emotional trauma can stay with us for a long time and affect us in many ways, as I've stated. It affects how we feel about ourselves and our belief to experience a current and future hope.

Thinking about your situation: -

- What has been the root cause of your anger?

- How high has been the intensity of the pain and rejection you've been feeling, on a scale of 1 to 10, with 10 being the highest?

- How have you responded to these challenges?

- How have you been able to help others, even when you've been in pain?

2. WHAT PHYSICAL CHALLENGES WAS HE FACING?

- How did Joseph decide to move forward?

- How did he say no to sexual temptation?

- How did he work things out from day to day?

- How did he let go and receive wholeness in every aspect of his life?

- How did he move into divine purpose while the pain of his past and the present situation was revealing something else?

3. WHOM WAS HE GOING TO FORGIVE?

As if what he went through wasn't hard enough, he knew his brothers sold him, abandoned him; that's something that you can't 'un-know'. So one of the hardest things Joseph had to do was to get to a place in his life, where he had to decide to forgive those who had hurt him. It wasn't just his brothers he had to forgive; it was also Potiphar's wife for falsely accusing him of trying to rape her. He also had to forgive the butler, whom he'd interpreted a dream for two years prior and who, when he was released, forgot about Joseph in prison.

Forgiveness is hard and it can be a long process. However, there does have to come a time when you do need to forgive, let go and embrace a new free space in your life, so that you can resolve the emotional challenges you have faced. So a part of the healing process is to consider the following areas:

- Whom was he going to forgive?
- Whom was he going to let go of?
- Whom was he going to embrace?
- How would he forgive himself?

Thinking about yourself:-

- Whom are you going to forgive?
- Whom are you going to let go of?
- Whom are you going to embrace?
- Do you need to forgive yourself?

There is always time for change and growth. If you choose to move forward or to stay still, you've still made a decision. Joseph had to come face-to-face with himself, like all of us have to at some point in our lives.

- He had to deal with his insecurities.
- He had to believe in God again.
- He had to trust God again.
- He had to trust his family again.
- He had to walk towards his destiny.

I have now learned that what I've gone through, no matter

how difficult, was to help others. To be honest, it is hard to admit, because it was horrible to go through. Yet, I refuse to have gone through so much in life for it to not bear some good fruit for me.

This book is some of that good fruit — a harvest I did not imagine. It was to bring hope to those of you who have ever felt like even life rejected you and was unfair to you. I hope you will find that your pathway is bright, with God's light to direct you to a place of restoration and hope, and give you the ability to come out of your maze, once and for all.

PATHWAYS TO HEALING:
Overcoming Childhood Trauma and Adult Pain of Sibling Estrangement

CHAPTER TWENTY-FIVE:
SILENT VOICES, HEAR ME ROAR

I mentioned earlier that I have over sixty unpublished poems. The following poem reminds me that we don't always have control of the twenty-four hours we have each day. Sometimes, we have too much to deal with in one day. I hope you enjoy it!

My Night & Day

Night and Day, 24 hours is enough to bear
Thank you for the moon and stars, sun and clouds that tag each other at the right time to shine
Night and Day, 24 hours is enough to share
My pain, my hurts, my concerns with You, Papa God
Thank You for hearing me all the time and for answering my prayers.

Thank You, LORD, that You are my Moon and Star,
Sun and Cloud, My Night and Day.

C. Carrol Poem *1990's*

If you were the last child, middle child or wherever you were born, then like me, you may have struggled to be heard. You had to fight every time to be noticed. In my case though, things were even more complicated. I was an intuitive child. I was very aware of other people's emotions and unspoken issues. I've mentioned this already, so what's your superpower? Despite this, I never did understand what made people sad. I could sense when people were not emotionally balanced or were upset. But I thought who, equally, was aware of my pain? So being an empath, I'm able to feel other people's pain as if it were my own. I know this can be hard at times, as if I didn't have enough to deal with already. I expand on this a bit more below.

However, one clear thing is that we all deal with emotional pain differently. Most times, we cover it up by working a lot and being busy, so we don't have to think about things. Some people suddenly become bossy and pick on others, making others feel small, so they can make themselves feel better. This usually involves the use of hurtful and demeaning words, manipulation and control. Drawing a comparison between what you see in people and what is happening in your life can mislead you. Just because someone is bubbly and has a cheery demeanour doesn't mean they're happy or living a better life than you.

You must know that everyone has something they're dealing with, no matter how small. As human beings, we don't like to show everyone our pain. So, stop looking at others and focus on the issues in your life; focus on finding a solution to your problems, so you can be equipped to help yourself.

Reflect on your life and ask:

- What have you been consistently experiencing in your life that has made you deeply sad when you think about it?

- Do you blame anyone for the problems you have experienced?

- What do you take responsibility for?

- How can you get back to a place of happiness?

Misplaced responsibility occurs when you carry an obligation that isn't yours. This is often a great cause of discomfort and worry. It causes you to question yourself, because the responsibility you carry isn't yours, so, you don't know what to do about it. It's like working at a job where you have no experience or the required skill set. That is what happens when you're in a situation where you have taken up responsibility for something that is not yours to bear. It causes you to doubt and blame yourself, even without any evidence that suggests you're at fault. If this isn't dealt with in time, you'll begin to condemn yourself. Your thoughts will be negative and self-defeating, and you'll think you're worthless.

PATHWAYS TO HEALING:
Overcoming Childhood Trauma and Adult Pain of Sibling Estrangement

We get into situations of misplaced priorities when people place expectations on us that aren't in any way ours. This is typical of how parents place huge expectations on their children, and consequently, the child begins to feel bad about themselves because they can't meet this expectation. They can grow up with low self-esteem and always striving to be accepted. But now, it is time for you to get out of this situation. Try to stop continuing to blame yourself for not fulfilling other people's expectations of you. You can take back what is yours and live, based on the goals you set for yourself. With help, you can stop and change the negative things you've been saying - statements like *"It is my fault"* or *"I should not have done that to provoke them"* - to more positive affirmations like *"I take responsibility for my life"* or *"I believe in myself."*

The weight of what others have placed on you will keep you stuck and stop you from fulfilling your destiny. I want you to know that it's your right to be healed and fulfilled in all areas of your life. If you continue to carry misplaced responsibility, you'll feel trapped. If you don't get out of it quickly, you'll start to associate with it as if it is normal. You will continue to be a people pleaser, and it can be difficult to move from here. So for me, over time my voice was becoming silent, to the point where

I felt like I had lost my voice for years, and so I didn't necessarily plan to write this book; it was a result of my journaling and expressing my experiences and desires. I started to empower myself back to health. Even though you feel there's no way out, let me tell you now that there is. Irrespective of what has happened, you have a way out. Just because those who were meant to care for you didn't, doesn't determine the total trajectory of your life. They didn't make you feel loved because they never felt loved themselves. They could not encourage you. And because they did not feel encouraged, remember all they did was only to bring you pain and disappointment. Despite all this, you must never give up. Never forget that you can have a mended heart. You can be happy and full of joy.

With help, please work through the feelings of guilt and worthlessness. They poison your mind with negative thoughts and that is what we want to avoid completely. The following extract is from an article by Dr Leslie Becker-Phelps in *Psychology Today*, explaining how to deal with feelings of guilt: 'People sometimes relate extremely well to someone else's pain and feel guilty for not alleviating it; even when they didn't cause the pain and it's not their responsibility to fix. They misinterpret their sadness, empathy, and their wish that they could help as a feeling of guilt. And they get unnecessarily *"tied up in knots"* with their distress.'

To determine if this is you, take a step back from your guilt, and do the following: Ask yourself, "What 'crime' did I commit?" For you to be guilty, you need to have done something wrong or harmful. Next, ask yourself, "Could I reasonably have known that my actions were wrong, or that a problem would ensue?" Committing a crime means that you choose to do something that you know is wrong or harmful. It is extremely important to understand that you can be responsible for a problem, or contributing to a problem, without being guilty. To help clarify this, let me share a personal example. Many years ago, I was driving home from work to a hospital, during twilight hours. I was driving within the speed limit through a local neighbourhood, when a large black dog sprinted in front of my car, and I unavoidably hit it. The dog eventually died, and I was wreaked with grief and guilt. However, I eventually realised that while I was responsible for killing the dog (there was no denying that I hit it with my car), I had not done anything that I could reasonably have known would cause such a horrible outcome. I was responsible, but not guilty. I admit that the distinction can be tricky, but it is key. Also, when you see someone suffering, it is important to ask yourself, "Is it my responsibility to fix the problem?

And, is it realistic for me to fix the problem?" You may truly want to fix things, or ease someone's pain, but this doesn't mean you are responsible for doing it, or guilty if you don't do it. Many problematic situations are too much for us to add to our load beyond what we can fix, or inappropriate for us to take on. You might be left feeling sad and sympathetic, which can be difficult emotions to experience. But turning them into guilt will only make you feel worse.

By thinking through your guilt and clarifying the situation, you might be able to end unnecessary distress. You might even free up more energy to help yourself and others - if only by openly listening to someone's distress, without having to defend yourself. You might also be better able to assist someone else in a way and at a pace that works for them, rather than pushing to fix things fast to alleviate your 'guilt.' So, if you are feeling guilty, pay close attention and ask yourself, *"Is it really guilt?"*

A possible way that you can stop feeling guilty is by identifying your abilities. When you do this, you identify what you can and cannot offer. And this helps you to recover from the feelings of guilt. To deal with guilt, we must notice what we're thinking: are our thoughts negative or positive? By thinking through your guilt and clarifying the situation, you will end unnecessary distress. Not only that, you will free up more energy to live a calmer life. In the next action steps, we will focus on the guilt you may be feeling, which is holding you back.

PATHWAYS TO HEALING:
Overcoming Childhood Trauma and Adult Pain of Sibling Estrangement

ACTION STEPS

What to Focus On

1. Are you experiencing misplaced guilt? Do others feel the brunt of your hurts?

2. What are you still being blamed for?

3. What things do you always have to defend?

4. What do you take responsibility for in your life?

CHAPTER TWENTY-SIX:
TRUTH BE TOLD

In life, we interact with people from day to day. Our first interaction and the first relationships we have are with our parents or carers. Then, as we grow, we begin to interact with family members and then with society. In all of these interactions, we'll clash with a few people from time to time. It can be a small argument and settled instantly, or a major issue that brings pain and misery for years. Dealing with family hurts is a major issue, as we tend to hold someone responsible for the hurt we feel. We can hold responsible the person in the prison of our mind, and vow never to interact with this person ever again. Are you holding someone in prison for something they did or did not do? Are they aware of how you feel? So ask and answer this question, or you might just be misplacing your blame.

From my experience, misplaced blame is damaging. The person is either not aware they've hurt you, doesn't even care, or it may even be that you're begrudging the wrong person. To avoid being caught up in this situation, always try and talk to the person you hold responsible for your hurt if you can. Although, I know that some of those who have hurt you may have died, so walking through the steps of forgiveness would help you move on. So whenever I would try to sort out an issue, most of the time I would be told by others, *"I don't know what you're talking about,"* and then I would feel like I had always misread the situation. It can be so exhausting. Often, we make ourselves vulnerable again and again to other people, because we want them to take responsibility for what they've done to us. But what do you do when others don't want to? We have to decide to let go and, where possible, forgive and move on with our lives, or the hurt will go on for longer than necessary. Think about it; you have a situation where you got hurt. You blame someone, but you could be blaming the wrong person(s); you can live your life in a rut that keeps pulling you down. So, you mustn't misplace your blame. We can hurt so deeply, that our perception can be blurry, and we can blame so many people for the hurt we've experienced, it's only when we get a clearer view of our situation that we're able to identify the persons(s) responsible, this will then set us free from all confusion.

The truth we know always sets us free. When you face and accept the truth, moving on becomes very easy. You drop all the baggage you've been carrying and you free up energy to pursue other life endeavours. By accepting the truth, you don't tie yourself to what hurts you anymore. You will not need those who hurt you to apologise or acknowledge what they did to you, because your life will be completely free from hurt. The steps towards being empowered include deciding how you choose to move forward, and facing the truth is very crucial to this process. The truth is that it's different for everyone; if you're unwilling to accept the truth, getting your life back will be impossible.

Hurt people must, in any way, shape or form, get healing so they can lead fulfilling lives. To heal, we have to learn to let go of things, especially things outside of our control. When you let go of things that hurt you, it enables you to redesign your life along the lines you want to follow. It gives you the power to become the captain of your life.

At this point, you become less susceptible to external influences. By doing so, you embrace your destiny with both hands. Your destiny is waiting for you to be ready for it, and it needs you to let go and move forward. The next poem was based on a decision to let go, to forgive and allow healing into my life, to no longer give any more of my time to those who don't love and appreciate me. You have to get to a point in your life where you draw a line in the sand, for your protection and sanity, and say ENOUGH IS ENOUGH!

To All

To all my haters, those who never understood me, liked me,

judged me and belittled me. To those who abused me with words, a look to the side, or who looked down on me. To all those who never understood me, to all those who placed

expectations on me that were not mine.
To all those who blamed me when it had
nothing to do with me.

To all those who would not love and accept me for me.
To all those who left me without a word. To all the liars, who twisted the truth to create a black cloud around my life, just to hide their experiences.

I forgive you!

I no longer hold the lie which stops the truth from shining through. See... there it is the light, the truth, the freedom.

Come join me.

C. Carrol *Poem*
Sept 2015

So, let's look at some more action steps to take through your maze to find out what new truths you can start believing.

ACTION STEPS

What do you believe?

1. What new truth do you now believe about yourself?
   _____
   _____
   _____
   _____

2. What new truths can you believe about your situation?
   _____
   _____
   _____
   _____

3. What does your new truth look like (Acceptance? Love?)?
   _____
   _____
   _____
   _____

PATHWAYS TO HEALING:
Overcoming Childhood Trauma and Adult Pain of Sibling Estrangement

CHAPTER TWENTY-SEVEN:
PATHWAYS TO HEALING

My healing journey took a long time. That's because, at one point, I did not know I had a problem, so I did not know anything needed to be fixed. But, after I opened myself to the truth about my situation and God's intervention, I started to see things more clearly. When you depend on your knowledge alone to understand what is happening to you and around you, it limits your breakthrough and perspective. It was then that I started to see the truth unravel about my life, and began to take steps towards healing. I did not know what the pathway to my healing looked like. Even now, I am still on that journey towards healing, but so much closer towards walking in a straight path back to me!

You will have found several different steps throughout this book that would help you get onto your path of healing, navigate through the maze, and get to the end and out of the cycle of hurt towards living a full life. What I can say is that healing might be a lifelong experience. Once you get used to it, you'll be able to deal with any situation that you come across.

PATHWAYS TO HEALING:
Overcoming Childhood Trauma and Adult Pain of Sibling Estrangement

There is always so much we can do towards our healing. My suggestion is to at least start moving forward and do something that will change your life. Don't just think, if I leave it, it will sort itself out; remember, you are now going to take one hundred per cent responsibility for your life. You have to play your part in your healing (I know you get that by now). So let's look again at some of the areas I've mentioned and I would like to offer five more areas that can help you start straight away, to help you get to the end of your maze:

- The first step is to **Acknowledge** that the abuse took place, and work through the emotions that come up for you. I mentioned that I had journaled my experiences for years, so maybe you can start writing down how you are feeling, and work through this with some external support.

- The second step is to **Grieve** the loss. I talked about the areas of famine you may have gone through, and it's OK to feel the loss, but don't get stuck there. We love our siblings; it's not that we hate them, it's just that there are times when we have to take time out to heal.

- So the third step is to remember the reason you need to **Heal**. It's easy to get back into relationships whilst the wounds are open and get hurt again. The gift of healing is what we give ourselves.

- The fourth step is to **Break past patterns**. Recognising the old patterns of behaviour you have with others is a big part of working towards changing the dynamics of the relationship. To heal, we have to know the old patterns to be able to break them. Becoming more aware of our actions and interactions with others, and how they interact with us, is key. This new revelation will lessen the negative reactions and enable you to think and act in a controlled manner.

So the fifth area is

- **Reclaim** – your life!!! Getting to a place in your life where you feel you can breathe again can be hard, but you can become more confident in your decisions and get back to a place where you build a stronger sense of self. Creating new boundaries lets others know you will not tolerate abuse anymore, which will make you less emotionally vulnerable and taken for granted in the future. OK, there is so much we can implement into our lives to help bring the change we long to have. Some can be simple activities we do daily; some take more work.

What will help you feel better about yourself and create new positive habits for your life? As not to overwhelm you, I've listed some more things you can consider. Below are nine holistic approaches, jam-packed with some fun and practical things you can implement in your life. It's a self-care approach that can bring some balance, healing and wholeness to your life. Creating new dynamics in your life opens new opportunities and new experiences into your everyday schedule.

PATHWAYS TO HEALING:
Overcoming Childhood Trauma and Adult Pain of Sibling Estrangement

1. HEALING

The last few years have seen me restored to my true self through the achievement of inner healing and several breakthroughs. I have been able to fix my self-esteem issues through God's help and counselling. To be honest, God has done so much for me throughout the process of my healing. Throughout my journey, I could feel God's love for me so much. I couldn't have healed without Him. I have found my freedom and purpose, and have achieved a lot during my journey. I find encouragement in the following words:

"When you pass through the waters, I will be with you; and when you pass through the rivers, they will not sweep over you. When you walk through the fire, you will not be burned; the flames will not set you ablaze. For I am the Lord your God, the Holy One of Israel, your Saviour" – Isaiah 43:2-3 (NIV).

I felt like I was passing through a river, and it was trying to drown me. So, to get your life back on track and walk in the light of God's Word, several things need to be done. Are you ready to make some more adjustments and improvements in the following aspects of your life? If yes, let's look at the areas that need focus, and create new paradigms in your life.

2. STRONG BODY

To have a strong body, we need to keep physically healthy. I enjoy my walks, as there are so many open spaces where I live and so much to explore. Apart from that, it's also my time for self-care. Our bodies were made to move around, so if you're not moving or exercising as much as you could, then set a plan to go out for an hour, take time to run, or take up a sports activity, and build your muscles. It also means getting enough sleep, keeping yourself hydrated and relieving stress. So looking after your body is key to overall health.

3. HEALTHY EMOTIONS

Our emotions need to be healthy, as negative emotions affect our lives, and so we need to have some positive and grounded things to implement into our thinking to enable us to enjoy life. We need to start building a healthy emotion, particularly when we've gone through so many traumatic experiences. It takes time and, just like we MOT our car, we need to maintain our emotions to remain healthy and whole. Neglecting your emotions, then, will only make you ineffective. You can take active steps to guide and nurture your feelings. If you feel distressed, you can do this through regular counselling sessions. Engage in fun activities that boost positive emotions, such as having something that makes you laugh out loud.

If you enjoy going to the movies, book a ticket to go, buy your popcorn and drink and go, or listen to upbeat or reflective music. Keeping a gratitude journal also helps balance your emotions, and focus on the changes taking place in your life every day.

4. BALANCED MIND

Next up are your cognitive abilities. Balanced mental stability is key to being able to move on from a hurtful past. Having something positive to look forward to is a good motivator. We need to start taking and enjoying our lives again on our terms, and to show up for ourselves because we're worth it. We need to improve our cognitive abilities through counselling, support groups, having a mentor or life coach, and reading and learning new things. It helps to also find time to laugh and then laugh some more. Equally, it's important to know what new interests you could enjoy now.

5. SOCIAL ACTIVITY

We grow as we build our social life. To help others - being kind, friendly and helpful - makes us relatable to other people. You may feel you don't have good social skills, but you can build your social skill set, get outside and meet people in small groups. Go for walks, enjoy the sun, and spend time with friends and family. Join a new activity that is of interest to you. Plan dates with your spouse and regular fun time with your children. Also, reduce the time spent on social media.

6. SPIRITUAL

We all need a balanced spiritual life; we need to build a relationship with God and other like-minded people. Start from where you are, reading and meditating on Scripture or other related books that will encourage and increase your faith, having devotions, and believing what it says about you. Enjoy your life, have fun. Engage with other Christians, and be part of a smaller cell group every week, to develop meaningful friendships and listen to uplifting music or worship songs.

7. YOUR HEALTH

Self-care will build your self-esteem, so have regular check-ups with the doctors and with your dentist; take a healthy detox cleanse; take the vitamins/supplements that can help you build a strong immune system; reduce your sugar intake; have a healthy and balanced diet, and have good body hygiene.

8. DAILY ROUTINES

Wake up early; have a routine for the day; have devotions and prayer time; create a meal plan; eat balanced meals; handle your finances; create budgets, and seek help when dealing with debts.

9. ASK FOR HELP

Once you start on the pathway to healing, life can become a very rewarding and relaxing process. As the layers of hurt start to unravel, you start to trust and hope again. It is just like a burst of energy that gets released. The heaviness starts to lift, and your mind starts to settle. Call it a soul detox, where you start letting go of everything and everyone, so you can feel free and enjoy the birth of fresh air. That is exactly what healing is.

In my experience, I went through several stages of forgiveness, prayers and individual ministry. Some of you may be aware of the ministry of Restoring the Foundations, and Sozo. Although these ministries focus on similar aspects, their delivery is different. So the focus is to help people identify any negative patterns in their upbringing, any ungodly beliefs or any past traumatic experiences that have kept us stuck and we can't seem to be free from. I've found that these ministries helped me tremendously to be free from my past and change the negative beliefs I had. I was also encouraged with the words of knowledge from a group of people who could relate to hearing from God on my behalf, and who gave me very encouraging words. And it was over time that the truth of the word started to diminish the lies about my circumstances.

10. HIS PLAN

Looking back at my life now, I've seen a lot of changes that have unfolded in different ways. I was always loved and I've never been alone, even when I felt lonely. Through my poems and drawings, He spoke to me. He gave me these abilities to help me cope with the hurt that was trying to eat me alive. He had a plan for my life and, now, it is beginning to manifest. I want to share with you a vision God showed me in 2017. It was so awesome that I was dumbfounded. In this vision, I saw a massive colour palette that filled the sky. In this image, I saw God going through my life, right back to the point where I was a young child. The image was moving very quickly, and it looked like several clouds in the sky moving at high speed. He was taking the palettes away from those people who had misused them to colour my life negatively. As He did this, all those palettes were disappearing into His palette. This was a very powerful revelation, and I didn't need much time to interpret what it was saying to me. God has the colour palette of my life. He will colour within the lines and place the right colours in my life. YES! Because He loves me that much! The acceptance of new truths opened and changed my perception in a liberating way. I think this Bible Scripture, which talks about what Jesus would do, was working on my behalf. It says in Luke 4:18-19 (NKJV) – *"The Spirit of the Lord is upon Me because He has anointed Me to preach the good news to the poor; He has sent Me to heal the broken-hearted, to proclaim liberty to the captives and recovery of sight to the blind, to set at liberty those who are oppressed, to proclaim the acceptable year of the Lord."*

As I began to allow God to take control of my life, I asked Him to give me sight. I prayed for Him to clean my eyes and change my perception, so I could see Him clearly and my circumstances, and to understand His plans for my life and to walk in it. He, as the loving Father He is, answered my prayers and I began living my life more freely, never to be bound by that deep pain anymore. You, too, can make a decision now. I chose to see: My Love, My Strength, My Joy, My Peace, My Beauty, My Forgiveness, My Uniqueness, My Life… And I know there is so much more to be seen. I am not my pain; it is something that happened to me. Although I was living in a constant state of pain, I chose that it will no longer define me. We should not get our identity from what we've been through, because God defines who we are. So let's look at the final action steps that will help towards creating new things, and that will empower and strengthen you to live your best life.

PATHWAYS TO HEALING

ACTION STEPS

Your Journey Steps

1. What new things will you do to empower yourself?

   _____
   _____
   _____
   _____

2. How will you start trusting yourself more?

   _____
   _____
   _____
   _____

3. What does love look like for you now?

   _____
   _____
   _____
   _____

4. What will you now do to express self-love and acceptance?

   _____
   _____
   _____
   _____

ACCEPTED IN THE BELOVED

We're reminded that we are accepted in the beloved:

Ephesians 1:5 (NLT) says, *'God decided in advance to adopt us into His own family by bringing us to Himself through Jesus Christ. This is what He wanted to do, and it gave Him great pleasure.'*

Jeremiah 30:17 (ESV) says *"'...I will restore health to you, and your wounds I will heal," declares the LORD, "because they have called you an outcast..."'*

So even if you've felt like you are not accepted into your biological family, God has enough room for you in His family, and this brings Him great pleasure. He promises to restore health to you, and heal your wounds. Isn't that wonderful? He wants you to be healed, He wants you to be well, and He wants you to be the best you.

I want to say to you, may you come out of the maze of confusion, disappointment, despair, rejection, abandonment, fear, blame and shame, and go forward and heal, so you can prosper and fulfil your destiny and purpose. You have always been strong; who else could have gone through what you've gone through? You have a purpose on Earth that only you can accomplish. And when you walk to the end of your path, use this new-found purpose to help others like you. Please do reach out to me, and let me know how you've walked through your pathways to your healing. There is one more poem I would like to encourage and share with you. It's entitled, *Strong!*

Strong!

*You are not strong in your strength.
You're strong because you allowed the greatness within you
to help you overcome your challenges.*

Poem C. Carrol 2019

PATHWAYS TO HEALING:
Overcoming Childhood Trauma and Adult Pain of Sibling Estrangement

Are you a dreamer, just like Joseph in the Bible? Are you carefree and enjoying your life? Joseph's story is well-known and highlights the power of a single dream. In one moment, his life is changed. Joseph experienced the hurt of betrayal from his brothers, who sold him into slavery.

Carmen shares her own story of experiencing sibling rejection. It began from the age of six, and it had an impact on her childhood and adult life. She draws lessons from Scripture to bring hope on how you can also walk through the maze of hurt, guilt, shame and confusion of past pain, and to overcome the challenges of today. She takes you on her journey of a painful experience that can bring the strongest person to their knees, and takes you to a place of self-love, forgiveness, hope and healing.

Carmen guides you through several pit stops in identifying the internal critic—those voices that pull you down and tell you that you are too sensitive. Learn how to change your inner dialogue and to walk on your Pathways to Healing.

ABOUT THE AUTHOR

Since she was a child, Carmen has always been creative—using her drawings and poetry to express herself to others. The last of eight siblings, she resides in Bristol, UK, and lives with her husband, Mel. She enjoys travelling and watching old movies. She is an empowerment speaker, and has contributed towards empowering women, using biblical teachings to improve every facet of their lives. She was a co-presenter on a community radio station for nine years, alongside her husband.

She used this platform to play uplifting music and share empowerment talks. Visit her marketing company at Patricia Rhema - http:// patriciarhema.com/ - to learn more. Also, for merchandise, visit https://carmen-carrol-enterprise.creator-spring.com/

Thanks for reading! I hope you found this book useful and encouraging. Please do leave a review on the site where you bought the book—much appreciated. To be informed on future books, sign up to my email list: http://carmencarrol.com

PATHWAYS TO HEALING:
Overcoming Childhood Trauma and Adult Pain of Sibling Estrangement

INDEX

Page 7 - Truth - John 8:32 - https://biblehub.com/john/8-32.htm
– Maze - https://dictionary.cambridge.org/dictionary/english/maze
Page 9 & 103 - Plans – Jeremiah 29:11 - https://biblehub.com/jeremiah/29-11.htm
Page 21 - Child – 1 Corinthians 13:11 – https://biblehub.com/1_corinthians/13-11.htm
Page 26 - Dr Ramani Durvasula - http://doctor-ramani.com/about/
– Psych2Go - https://psych2go.net/
– Dr Henry Cloud - https://www.drcloud.com/
- Beverly Engel http://healmyshame.com/
– Narcissistic - Rethink.org - https://www.rethink.org/advice-and-information/about-mental-illness/learn-more-about-conditions/personality-disorders/
Page 26 & 103 - Destroy & Abundant life – John 10:10 – https://biblehub.com/niv/john/10.htm
Page 28 - Live – Ezekiel 16:4-6 - https://biblehub.com/bsb/ezekiel/16.htm
Page 30 – Jacob & Esau - Genesis 25:19-34 - https://biblehub.com/genesis/25-22.htm
– Jacob & Esau story overview https://biblehub.com/library/anonymous/wee_ones_bible_stories/jacob_and_esau.htm
Page 33 - Power – http://dictionary.reference.com/browse/power
Page 11 - Rejection – https://en.oxforddictionaries.com/definition/rejection
Page 15 - Refresh – Psalms 23:3 - https://biblehub.com/psalms/23-3.htm

PATHWAYS TO HEALING:
Overcoming Childhood Trauma and Adult Pain of Sibling Estrangement

Page 16&39 - Psalms 139:15-16 - https://biblehub.com/psalms/139-15.htm
Page 17 – Rebuke - Proverbs 27:5-6 - https://biblehub.com/proverbs/27-5.htm
Page 29 - Offended Brother – Proverbs 18:19-20 – https://biblehub.com/proverbs/18-19.htm
Page 34 - Sow - Psalms 126:5 - https://biblehub.com/psalms/126-5.htm
Page 16&39 - Psalms 139:15-16 - https://biblehub.com/psalms/139-15.htm
Page 35 – Heals - Psalms 147:3 - https://biblehub.com/psalms/147-3.htm
Page 40 - Strong– Deuteronomy 31:6 – https://biblehub.com/deuteronomy/31-6.htm
Page 51 - Condemnation - Romans 8:1-2 - https://biblehub.com/romans/8-1.htm
– Beauty - Isaiah 61:3 - https://biblehub.com/bsb/isaiah/61.htm
Page 52- Les Brown – Quote - https://www.azquotes.com/quote/1318331
Page 54 & 116 - Romans 8:28 – https://www.biblegateway.com/passage/?search=Romans%208:28
Page 55 - Psalms 34:4-5 - https://biblehub.com/psalms/34-4.htm
– Psalms 34:18 - Lord - https://biblehub.com/psalms/34-18.htm
– 2 Corinthians 10:5 - https://biblehub.com/2_corinthians/10-5.htm
– Henry Ford - https://www.goodreads.com/quotes/978-whether-you-think-you-can-or-you-think-you-can-t--you-re
Page 56 - Control – https://www.google.com/search?q=control+meaning&oq=control+meaning&aqs=chrome..69i57.5630j0j7&sourceid=chrome&ie=utf-8
Page 56 - Pain - https://www.oxfordlearnersdictionaries.com/definition/english/pain_1

INDEX

Page 60 - God Speaks - Job 33:14-18(NIV) - http://biblehub.com/niv/job/33.htm

Page 64 - Joseph story - Genesis 37:1-4 – https://biblehub.com/niv/genesis/37.htm

– Hate- Oxford Dictionary - https://www.oxfordlearnersdictionaries.com/definition/english/hate_1

Page 65 – Garden – https://www.oxfordlearnersdictionaries.com/definition/english/garden_1

– Noble – https://www.oxfordlearnersdictionaries.com/definition/english/noble_1

– Warrior - https://www.google.com/search?q=meaning+Warrior&oq=meaning+Warrior&aqs=chrome..69i57.4131j0j7&sourceid=chrome&ie=UTF-8

Page 65 - Hate - Psalm 69:4 - https://biblehub.com/psalms/69-4.htm

Page 67 – Decide Job 22:28 - https://biblehub.com/job/22-28.htm

– I Am – Billy Graham– https://billygraham.org/decision-magazine/february-2008/the-i-ams-of-jesus

Page 68 – I am – Bread - https://biblehub.com/john/6-35.htm

– I am Light – John 8:12 – https://biblehub.com/john/8-12.htm

– I am the door - John 10:9 – https://biblehub.com/john/10-9.htm

– I am the Good Shepherd – John 10:11 – https://biblehub.com/john/10-11.htm

– I am Resurrection – John 11:25 – https://biblehub.com/john/11-25.htm

– I am the way - John 14:6 - https://biblehub.com/john/14-6.htm

– I am Vine – John 15:1 – https://biblehub.com/john/15-1.htm

– I am the door - https://biblehub.com/john/10-9.htm

Page 71 - Dream - Genesis 37:5-11– https://biblehub.com/bsb/genesis/37.htm

Page 73 - Destiny - http://www.thefreedictionary.com/destiny

PATHWAYS TO HEALING:
Overcoming Childhood Trauma and Adult Pain of Sibling Estrangement

Page 74 - Jesus and Joseph comparisons - https://jewsforjesus.org/publications/newsletter/newsletter-sep-1985/a-comparison-between-joseph-and-jesus
– Father's Love – Genesis 37:3 –
https://biblehub.com/genesis/37-3.htm
– Matthew 3:17 – https://biblehub.com/matthew/3-17.htm
Page 75 - Stripped - Genesis 37:23 -
https://biblehub.com/genesis/37-23.htm
– Betrayed - Genesis 37:4 – https://biblehub.com/genesis/37-4.htm
– Hated - John 15:25 – https://biblehub.com/john/15-25.htm
– Pit - Genesis 37:24 – https://biblehub.com/genesis/37-24.htm
– Matthew 12:40 - https://biblehub.com/matthew/12-40.htm
– Plotted – Genesis 37:18 – https://biblehub.com/genesis/37-18.htm
– Crucify – Luke 23:21– https://biblehub.com/luke/23-21.htm
– Prison– Genesis 39:20 – https://biblehub.com/genesis/39-20.htm
– Crucified– Luke 23:33 – https://biblehub.com/luke/23-33.htm
– Led People - Genesis 41:41 -
https://biblehub.com/genesis/41-41.htm
– Philippians 2:9 - https://biblehub.com/philippians/2-9.htm
– Redeemed - Genesis 50:20 -
https://biblehub.com/genesis/50-20.htm
– Titus 2:14 - https://biblehub.com/titus/2-14.htm
– Matthew 27:28 – https://biblehub.com/matthew/27-28.htm
– Pit - Genesis 37:24 – https://biblehub.com/genesis/37-24.htm
Page 76 - Revelation - Genesis 45:3 –
https://biblehub.com/genesis/45-3.htm
– Romans 11:26 – https://biblehub.com/romans/11-26.htm
– Authority - Genesis 45:9 – https://biblehub.com/genesis/45-9.htmv
– Matthew 28:18 - https://biblehub.com/matthew/28-18.htmv
Page 77 & 114 – Brothers – Genesis 37:12-36 –
https://biblehub.com/bsb/genesis/37.htm

INDEX

Page 87 - Womb – Jeremiah 1:5 – https://biblehub.com/jeremiah/1-5.htm
– Fine – http://www.urbandictionary.com/define.php?term=fine
Page 89 - Depression – https://www.rethink.org/diagnosis-treatment/conditions/depression/about
– Anxiety – Proverbs 12:25 – https://biblehub.com/proverbs/12-25.htm
Page 95 - Ephesians 6:10-18 – https://biblehub.com/ephesians/6-10.htm
– Armour – Ephesians 6:16 – https://biblehub.com/ephesians/6-16.htm
Page 97 – Weights – http://biblehub.com/hebrews/12-1.htm
Page 99 – Proverbs 23:7 - https://biblehub.com/proverbs/23-7.htm
– New Heart - Ezekiel 36:26 – https://biblehub.com/ezekiel/36-26.htm
Abuse – http://www.thefreedictionary.com/abuse
Pae 102 – Dr Henry Cloud - Boundaries - https://www.boundariesbooks.com/
Page 107 – Grace - https://billygraham.org.uk/answer/what-is-grace-in-your-view/
Page 109 - Katie Souza - https://katiesouza.com/
Page 116 – Rejected - Isaiah 53:3 - https://biblehub.com/isaiah/53-3.htm
– Restore - Joel 2:25 - https://biblehub.com/joel/2-25.htm
Page 126 - Dr Leslie Becker-Phelps - https://www.psychologytoday.com/gb/blog/making-change/201209/when-guilt-is-good-and-when-its-misplaced
Page 136 - Isaiah 43:2 - https://biblehub.com/isaiah/43-2.htm
Page 138 – Anointed Luke 4:18 - https://biblehub.com/luke/4-18.htm
Page 140 - Ephesians 1:5 - https://biblehub.com/ephesians/1-5.htm

PATHWAYS TO HEALING:
Overcoming Childhood Trauma and Adult Pain of Sibling Estrangement

– Restore- Jeremiah 30:17 –
http://biblehub.com/esv/jeremiah/30-17.htm
Page 142- Restoring the Foundations -
https://restoringthefoundations.uk/

www.ingramcontent.com/pod-product-compliance
Lightning Source LLC
Chambersburg PA
CBHW072152100526
44589CB00015B/2190